Divine Healing in The Holy Scriptures: God's Mercy Towards Man

Chris A. Legebow

ISBN- 978-1-988914-02-2

DEDICATION

I thank God for the healing evangelists that have encouraged my life. The gifts of faith, healing and the working of miracles are gifts of the Holy Spirit in the earth to day in the body of Christ.

CONTENTS

ACKNOWLEDGMENTS

All scripture taken from Bible Gateway.com
Modern English Version (MEV)

1 MAN WAS CREATED TO LIVE ETERNALLY

Chapter 1

Man was created without sin, sickness or death

God created Adam and Eve and gave them the garden of Eden as a place to live. In it was every type of fruit tree. There were no weeds; there was no sin; they had God's companionship. They spoke with God. There were instructed that they could have any of the fruit of all the trees except one – the tree of the knowledge of good and evil. God told them that if they were to take from this tree, they would surely die.

Genesis 2: 15 The Lord God took the man and put him in the garden of Eden to till it and to keep it. 16 And the Lord God commanded the man, saying, "Of every tree of the garden you may freely eat, 17 but of the tree of the knowledge of good and evil you shall not eat, for in the day that you eat from it you will surely die."

The serpent possessed by Satan contradicted God's word. The serpent caused Eve, and Adam with her, to doubt God's words, to doubt what God had said isn't true and that the tree would make them wise as gods. Eve sees the fruit and covets it. She partakes of it and gives some to Adam who is with her.

Genesis 3: 3 Now the serpent was more subtle than any beast of the field which the Lord God had made. And he said to the woman, "Has God said, 'You shall not eat of any tree of the garden'?"

Genesis 3: 4 Then the serpent said to the woman, "You surely will not die! 5 For God knows that on the day you eat of it your eyes will be opened and you will be like God, knowing good and evil."

The Forbidden Fruit

They partake of the fruit of the forbidden tree. Immediately consequences occur. They do not instantly physically die but they instantly spiritually die. They realize they are naked. They cover themselves with leaves to hide their nakedness. They fear God rather than desire to speak to him as usual. They have changed because spiritually they can no longer connect with God in the same way because they have sinned. Spiritually they are separated from God. It has consequence not only for Adam and Eve but all of the earth. It affects their children; it affects all of humans and animals on the earth because they had been given authority over all the animals. They are also sentenced to die physically. I believe had they not sinned, humans would never die. The woman lusted after the fruit. She saw it looked desirable: the lust of the eyes; It was pleasing to her, the lust of the flesh. She thought upon the lie of the serpent that said it would make her as wise as god; the pride of life motivated her;

1 John 2: 16 For all that is in the world—the lust of the flesh, the lust of the eyes, and the pride of life—is not of the Father, but is of the world.

Genesis 3: 6 When the woman saw that the tree was good for food, that it was pleasing to the eyes and a tree desirable to make one wise, she took of its fruit and ate; and she gave to her husband with her, and he ate. 7 Then the eyes of both were opened, and they knew that they were naked. So they sewed fig leaves together and made coverings for themselves.

As part of the judgement on their sin, willful disobedience to God, Adam and Eve are banished from the Garden. They have tragedy in their family as one child murders the other. They no longer have close communion with God. For several hundred years that follow, no one is mentioned in their family of having any faith towards God. An absence of mentioning God means they were not in communion with God anymore. God pronounces Judgement on the serpent, the woman and the man. Their judgement affects all of the earth and all life on the earth; it continues to do so and will until Jesus Christ returns.

Death is a result of the curse upon Adam.

Also there is judgement on the serpent and on the woman. Woman was created as equal to the man, but because of the curse of sin, he will rule over her. She lost the freedom to be his equal. Because of her, there is pain in child bearing. If she had not sinned, it would not be as such. Her offspring would be at enmity with the serpent and one day, one of her descendants would crush the serpent`s head to end the curse of sin and its consequences.

Genesis 3:
15 I will put enmity
between you and the woman,

and between your offspring and her offspring;
he will bruise your head,
and you will bruise his heel."

16 To the woman He said,
"I will greatly multiply your pain in childbirth,
and in pain you will bring forth children;
your desire will be for your husband,
and he will rule over you."

Judgement on Adam

Death – with it comes sickness, disease, sin and consequences of it. The earth is cursed because of it. There are thorns and thistles and weeds. Life for Adam is toil rather than ease. Rather than simply pick the fruit from the trees that God had planted, they must remove the weeds, till the ground, sow seed and water it so that can grow. Also with the sentence of work comes the ending of life for all humans. There will be death eventually. It is a consequence of sin. It is as God told Adam – if they sinned, they would die.

Genesis 3: Cursed is the ground on account of you;
in hard labor you will eat of it
all the days of your life.
18 Thorns and thistles it will bring forth for you,
and you will eat the plants of the field.
19 By the sweat of your face
you will eat bread
until you return to the ground,
because out of it you were taken;
for you are dust,
and to dust you will return."

Adam's People

For almost 300 years, the lineage of Adam was a sinful people. Because Adam had lost communion with God, no one knew God. People became very wicked. In Genesis 6, it states that evil angels were having sexual relations with women and bearing children. It seems like horrible wickedness in itself, but it is more sinful than many people may understand.

Satan was cast out of heaven for the sin of pride, for not wanting to give glory to God, and for considering himself equal to God. Lucifer, now named Satan, was a covering angel over God. His responsibility was to give all the praise and worship and glory to God. One day, pride arose in his heart and he chose to keep the glory himself. He had been a beautiful creature made to give God glory, but because of his sin, he was thrown out of heaven into the atmosphere of the earth. One third of the angels chose to go with him rather than serve God.

Ezekiel 28: 13 You were in Eden,
  the garden of God;
every precious stone was your covering:
  the sardius, topaz, and the diamond,
  the beryl, the onyx, and the jasper,
  the sapphire, the emerald, and the carbuncle, and gold.
The workmanship of your settings and sockets was in you;
  on the day that you were created, they were prepared.
14 You were the anointed cherub that covers,
  and I set you there;
you were upon the holy mountain of God;
  you walked up and down in the midst of the stones of fire.
15 You were perfect in your ways
  from the day that you were created,
  until iniquity was found in you.
16 By the multitude of your merchandise,
  you were filled with violence in your midst,
  and you sinned;
therefore I have cast you as profane out of the mountain of God;

Pride

The sin of pride that started with Satan, was the same sin that Adam and Eve committed as they doubted God's words and desired to be made as gods knowing good from evil. Adam and Eve were never meant to know evil. Evil is not something originating with God. Satan is the originator of sin against God. Adam and Eve willfully sinned against God. Later in their lineage, because they had cut off their relationship with God, their descendants are so wicked that they are choosing sexual relations with demons. That means their wickedness was such that they did not even consider God any more. Rather, they chose the evil angels and did not even seek God.

God had made man (and woman) in the image of God: spirit, soul and body. Scripture calls humans the crowning glory of God's creation.

Psalm 8:
4 what is man that You are mindful of him,
and the son of man that You attend to him?
5 For You have made him a little lower than the angels,
and crowned him with glory and honor.
6 You have given him dominion over the works of Your hands;
You have put all things under his feet,

God created humans to have communion with Him – to be his friends. God created man as a companion for Himself. Man was created to be holy and to live in the glory of God's presence. The turning of mankind towards the demons rather than God is humans living the opposite of how we were created to live. We were meant to live in the holy presence of God, knowing the blessings of God. Adam's curse – produced an evil offspring. They were so wicked with violence, hatred, sexual immorality and other such sins that God chose to destroy them and all the creatures of the earth because of it. [The wicked angels who sinned were bound and placed in the center of the earth awaiting judgement (Revelation 9: 14). They will be released at the end of the age.]

God's judgement on the evil people in Genesis – impacts all the earth. Adam's sin impacted the whole earth.

Sin entered the world through Adam; communion with God was cut off. For hundreds of years, God waited for a person who desired to commune with him. Enoch is mentioned and so is Noah. Enoch was taken from the earth – literally- because he knew and loved God.

Genesis 5: 22 Enoch walked with God after the birth of Methuselah for three hundred years and had other sons and daughters. 23 So all the days of Enoch were three hundred and sixty-five years. 24 Enoch walked with God, and then he was no more because God took him.

God made covenant with Noah.

Genesis 6: 8 But Noah found grace in the eyes of the Lord.
9 These are the generations of Noah.
Noah was a just man and blameless among his contemporaries. Noah walked with God. 10 Noah had three sons: Shem, Ham, and Japheth

Noah is the only family mentioned as being faithful or good. All of the other people were in terrible sin and wickedness on earth – violence, sexual immorality, hatred, evil God destroys the earth as it is known by a global flood. He shows mercy on Noah and his family and the animals. 2 of a kind of most animals, and 7 of a kind of other animals are spared as Noah builds a huge ark to keep them during the storm that is to come. Noah and his sons build the ark for 120 years. Noah is preaching to the people that God said it would rain. It had never rained before. No one besides Noah family believed. Their lives are saved as well as all the animals in the ark.

Noah offered a sacrifice

Noah offered a sacrifice to God in thanksgiving. God made covenant with Noah and all the animals and all the earth that He would never again destroy all people and animals. Covenant is a promise that God makes with people. God always keeps His word. He promised Noah and the animals of the earth that He would place his rainbow in the sky as a symbol of His promise.

Genesis 8: 20 Then Noah built an altar to the Lord and took of every clean animal and of every clean bird and offered burnt offerings on the altar.

God's covenants originate with God. He seeks someone who wants to know God. He causes them to come to know Him. He chooses them and makes covenant promises to them – promises that not only affect them but all the generations after them. Even though there were not many people seeking God, God was making covenants with people as a way to restore His relationship with man. Revelation 13: 8 gives us the insight that God knew man was going to sin, so He made a way, before Adam was on earth. God gave Jesus as the solution before He created Adam. What is amazing is that God still desired to commune with man. Even though there are people who want nothing to do with Him, He still loves them and has provided an offering for sin as He promised He would do. God would never force Adam and Eve to obey Him even though it meant they would turn against Him.

God made covenant with others also: Abraham, Moses, and King David. God made special agreements with these people and although none of them is sinless, all of them desired to live for God and served God. They would offer animals as a sacrifice to God for their sin. Their sin was not erased, it was simply covered over. What they longed for was the day that Jesus Christ would come as Messiah and shed His blood as atonement or payment for Adam's sin.

The covenants were not in isolation. They are cumulative. That is they applied to the person and his family and also to all of his descendants. His covenant with Abraham was that Abraham would begin a mighty nation, a people so tremendous, a people of faith would serve God, they would be as many as stars in the sky or grains of sand on a beach.

His covenant with King David was that He would raise up David`s descendants (also descendants of Abraham, Isaac and Jacob, or Israel) to sit on the throne. He would establish them as kings in Israel. His blessing was on David`s lineage. Even though some of his descendants were exceedingly wicked, God had mercy on them because of His covenant with David. Jesus Christ comes from the lineage of David.

The covenant God made with Moses was a covenant for all of Israel. Israel is the people become a nation of people that God had promised to Abraham. Israel was chosen by God because they desired God and they served God. Through Moses God delivered Israel out of Egyptian captivity (after 400 years of it) and brought about 2 million Israelites through the midst of the Red Sea to a place He had promised them also the place promised to Abraham. Through Moses, we have the commandments of God. God chose Moses to lead Israel and to assure that the Levites or God`s chosen people as priests, would serve God in the manner that God chose.

Moses is not the origin of Judaism; Jehovah God is the origin of Judaism. God spoke directly to Moses and gave him the plans for building a tabernacle or place of worship. God instructed Moses and got Moses to write the 613 commandments of the Levitical laws that apply to every aspect of human life so that we would know God`s will for all people. God gave instruction about animal sacrifice as a covering for sin until the Messiah would be born. That was the offspring promised who would come, and redeem Israel from the curse of Adam. Thousands of years passed; there were good kings, evil kings and Israel was captured by Rome. Israel was once more no longer free.

Jesus the Messiah

It is in the Roman occupation of Israel that God brings the Messiah. It is not with grandeur or earthly authority that Jesus came to be King of Israel. He was a descendent of David, but he was born into a normal working-class family. All aspects of his birth are intertwined with the supernatural. All of these factors could be the study of a book by themselves; they are only mentioned here to show that Jesus truly is the Messiah promised. He fulfilled all Messianic prophecies.

Only Jesus could do what He did. He was born of the Virgin Mary (Luke 1: 35 – 38). He lived a Holy life without sin (Hebrews 4: 15). He died to pay the penalty for our sin.

Isaiah 53:
4 Surely he has borne our grief
  and carried our sorrows;
Yet we esteemed him stricken,
  smitten of God, and afflicted.
5 But he was wounded for our transgressions,
  he was bruised for our iniquities;
the chastisement of our peace was upon him,
  and by his stripes we are healed.

He died. He rose from the dead and ascended into heaven. (Matthew 28: 5-7) (Acts 1: 9)

Jesus fulfilled all the requirements for Adam's payment of sin. He defeated death, hell and the grave (Colossians 2: 15) Because of Jesus blood shed for us, we can be saved. Our salvation means we can be restored to God. We can commune with God once more. We can be the friends of God living a holy life because of Jesus blood. This in itself is worth shouting about. God saved us so we no longer have to live under the curse of Adam. All Christians believe the truth that Jesus Christ is the Messiah; Jesus Christ is our redeemer. Because of Jesus, our sins can be forgiven. If we will believe in Jesus , we can have relationship with God and eternal life.

Jesus atonement for sin was to cleanse the sin of Adam to make atonement for it. Saying that you are a Christian is part of being a Christian. Our words express our faith in God. Our words affirm Jesus Christ as LORD.

Romans 10: [d] This is the word of faith that we preach: 9 that if you
confess with your mouth Jesus is Lord, and believe in your heart that God
has raised Him from the dead, you will be saved, 10 for with the heart one
believes unto righteousness, and with the mouth confession is made unto
salvation.

Jesus Sacrifice Once and for all

Unlike the animal sacrifices that covered over people`s sins for thousands of years after the sin of Adam, Jesus shed His blood only once for all people who ever lived, are living or ever would live. Because Jesus` death, burial, resurrection and ascension into heaven, our sins are completely cleansed if we will believe in Jesus and what He did. Faith is the key ingredient. We must believe that what Jesus said is true and that the Scriptures that talk about «him are true. All of our salvation hangs on the one aspect: faith in Jesus Christ.

Hebrews 10: 10 By this will we have been sanctified through the offering of the body of Jesus Christ once for all.

Hebrews 10: 12 But this Man, after He had offered one sacrifice for sins forever, sat down at the right hand of God. 13 Since that time He has been waiting for His enemies to be made His footstool. 14 For by one offering He has forever perfected those who are sanctified.
Death upon all because of Adam – faith and redemption because of Jesus Christ.

1 Corinthians 15: There is a natural body, and there is a spiritual body. 45 So it is written, "The first man Adam was made a living soul."[c] The last Adam was made a life-giving spirit. 46 However, that which is spiritual is not first, but the natural, and then the spiritual. 47 The first man was of the earth, made of dust; the second man was the Lord from heaven. 48 As was the man of dust, so are those who are of dust; and as is the man of heaven, so are those who are of heaven. 49 As we have borne the image of the man of dust, we shall also bear the image of the man of heaven.

All Christians believe the scriptures above and believe they are saved because of Jesus sacrifice. They take the scriptures literally by faith and receive the free gift of eternal life through Jesus Christ. Many people who are Christians do not know the simple but profound truth that Jesus not only saves, but heals and delivers.

Jesus saved us by His blood. Jesus also took upon Himself all of the curse of sin which included sickness and disease. His blood was shed to make us free. I mean true freedom from all sin, or sickness or addiction or desire for evil. If we truly turn to Jesus Christ, we can experience communion with God much as Adam and Eve did before they sinned. We can speak to God and God will speak to us.

We can know that God hears our prayers. We can know what it is like to live Holy unto God. We can choose to live for God. Rather than be in bondage to sin, we can freely choose. True Christians daily make the decision to live for God. With free will, we choose God. It is the opposite of what Adam did. It is choosing to live obeying God because we honour

Him as God and we worship Him as God. We treasure our relationship with God. Rather than choose any other way, we believe God.

If you can believe that Jesus died for your sins, you can be saved. It is the same faith that believes in salvation, that can believe for healing. Jesus took the penalty upon Himself so that we might literally be healed. The curse upon Adam was that he would die. The curse of breaking the laws of Moses was sickness, poverty, living in the curse of Adam. Messiah has come. He has cleansed us; He is the same God that can bring healing to you. He redeemed us from the penalty of sin.

Christians must have faith to believe the scriptures literally mean healing, and you can be healed. O healing can come in so many ways. It can come no those who don`t even know Jesus. Once they are healed, they desire to serve Jesus. I have witnessed through television broadcasting Crusades preaching healing and miracles. I have seen people who are healed because of Jesus. They repent and give their lives to be Christians after their healing. If a non-believer can believe a preacher`s sermon and be healed by Jesus, a Christian should be even more able to receive healing knowing how good God is.

JESUS died for our healing

Jesus fulfilled these Messianic prophecies.

Isaiah 53: 4 Surely he has borne our grief
 and carried our sorrows;
Yet we esteemed him stricken,
 smitten of God, and afflicted.
5 But he was wounded for our transgressions,
 he was bruised for our iniquities;
the chastisement of our peace was upon him,
 and by his stripes we are healed.

Literally the words “ by his stripes we are healed”. Because Jesus suffered and died, we can have healing. It is faith in Jesus Christ, the same Jesus that died for your sins, that ignites faith to believe for healing. This includes spiritual life, healing in the inner person or soul as well as physical healing. Literally believe the word of God. Say it over yourself. `By Jesus stripes, I am healed.` Literally believe God`s Word. Jesus Christ is the same yesterday, today and forever. (Hebrews 13: 8)

Jesus commanded His disciples to preach salvation, healing and deliverance.

The same healing Jesus who lived on the earth has given believers authority to preach salvation, healing and deliverance. The Apostle Peter preaches Jesus Christ and gives Him all the glory for the man healed. After the disciples are filled with the Holy Spirit and baptized in the Holy Spirit, they have boldness to share the truths of Jesus Christ in public. The moving of the Holy Spirit upon them was so strong, it compelled them to go into the streets of Jerusalem where they were witnessed speaking in other tongues, some of them speaking earthly languages they had never learned. Because of their boldness to preach Jesus, thousands are saved that day and the Church of the testament multiplies.

Acts 2: 38 Peter said to them, "Repent and be baptized, every one of you, in the name of Jesus Christ for the forgiveness of sins, and you shall receive the gift of the Holy Spirit. 39 For the promise is to you, and to your children, and to all who are far away, as many as the Lord our God will call."

With the same boldness that the Apostle Peter preaches salvation to the multitudes, He preaches Jesus Christ the Healer. He exalts the name of Jesus and gives God glory by doing it.

Acts 3: 16 And His name, by faith in His name, has made this man strong, whom you see and know. And faith which comes through Him has given him perfect health in your presence.

Acts 4: 8 Then Peter, filled with the Holy Spirit, said to them, "Rulers of the people and elders of Israel: 9 If we today are being examined concerning a good deed done to a crippled man, how this man has been healed, 10 be it known to you all, and to all the people of Israel, that by the name of Jesus Christ of Nazareth, whom you crucified, whom God raised from the dead, by Him this man stands before you whole.

Even though the disciples healed people, doing what no one else was doing, giving God glory and using the name of Jesus as the authority, many religious rulers hated them and beat them and threw them in jail. Even though they were persecuted for their faith in the name of Jesus, they continued to do it. They did it because they knew that they knew the same Jesus who healed people while He was on earth, still heals people through the Holy Spirit that lives within them. They acknowledged Jesus as the healer. They gave the glory to God. That is the sign of a true Christian. True Christians will magnify and exalt the LORD Jesus Christ. They will know that only God can heal. Only God can receive the glory.

2 DIVINE HEALTH, DIVINE HEALING GOD'S WILL

Chapter 2 Divine Health and Healing is God's Will

Healing and miracles occurred in the Old Covenant. God made special provisions in the Levitical laws instructing people how to give an offering of thanksgiving for being healed. God's promises to Moses and the children of Israel were such that they would live in health and live long joyful lives. In some instances of healing, prophets of God were used to release a special word that brought healing or long life. Divine healing is for all people not only Christians. Those who do not know God turn to Him after they are healed.. God will heal people who are not believers if they will have faith to believe and obey the servant of God being used.

After a thorough reading of the book of Leviticus and the book of Deuteronomy, a person will surely see the scriptures about health and long life as results of serving God and keeping the commandments. God's plan is that his people should live long and prosper during their lives. He promised it to Moses and Joshua. He promised it through Psalms and proverbs. If God's people will seek him and serve him with all their lives, they can expect blessings such as health and long life.

Long Life

God's will is to heal – these are some of the promises of blessings upon Israel. The release of the blessings of God towards people cover all aspects of human life: physical, spiritual, and of the soul. God commands us to keep His word as the priority and to cherish it and keep it constantly. That is to pray it, to read it, to magnify His Word so that all we see is in light of the Word of God. To let the Word of God be the primary motivation for our hands; that we would do the Word of God. God instructs us to keep the Word of God in our hearts as the plumb line by which all things are measured.

Deuteronomy is especially written to Israel so that they will always keep God's Word because His Word expresses His will for us. It is essential in keeping relationship with God. God says that is we will keep His commandments, He will bless us. Blessing means provision, protection, fertility, prosperity, abundance, joy, peace, the benefits of the covenant are many. All of Deuteronomy mentions very specific natural blessings and provisions. God is a prosperity preacher. Blessings cover relationships, animals, career, creative works, business, favour with people, receiving special favour from people because you are God's chosen people.

Deuteronomy 28: 28 Now it will be, if you will diligently obey the voice of the Lord your God, being careful to do all His commandments which I am commanding you today, then the Lord your God will set you high above all the nations of the earth. 2 And all these blessings will come on you and overtake you if you listen to the voice of the Lord your God.

To King Solomon, God spoke a special blessing because God asked him what he would want from God and Solomon asked for wisdom to rule the people. Because his heart was not selfish, God honoured him and made him the wisest king who ever lived. He gave him all types of blessings such as possessions, wealth and honour.

2 Chronicles 1: 11 Then God responded to Solomon, "Because this was in your heart and you did not ask for possessions, wealth, and honor, or even the life of those who hate you, nor have you asked for many days of life, but you have asked Me for wisdom and knowledge that you might govern My people over whom I have made you king, 12 wisdom and knowledge are now given to you. Possessions, wealth, and honor I will also give to you; such has not been given to kings before you nor those who will follow after you."

God promises long life to those who seek him for wisdom. The theme of putting God's word first is throughout all of the scriptures, because it is the main point the Holy Spirit wants to impress to us who read the Bible. It spans all of the 66 books. Knowing God's will is essential in keeping God's will. Doing God's will, is a choice we can make to honour God, to live a life that is blessed and abundant and joyful. He promises long life to those who keep the teachings of the Word of God.

Proverbs 3: 3 My son, do not forget my teaching,
but let your heart keep my commandments;
2 for length of days and long life
and peace will they add to you.

Length of days and peace come through keeping God's commandments. Godly wisdom is to be sought. It is the opposite of what

Adam and Eve were seeking when they disobeyed God and took from the tree of good and evil. Godly wisdom is seeking only God's wisdom – not the knowledge of evil. Godly wisdom is specifically given these qualities defined by God. Pure means there is no evil or no wrong doing. It brings peace. Strife or fighting is the direct opposite of God's wisdom. God's wisdom can bring peace. It is gentle. It is never forced upon someone. It is merciful and kind with good fruits (Gal 5: 22- 26) and is not only for certain people but to all who will believe. It doesn't contradict itself.

James 3: 17 But the wisdom that is from above is first pure, then peaceable, gentle, open to reason, full of mercy and good fruits, without partiality, and without hypocrisy

Godly wisdom is an important part of the blessing of God because it helps a person in all areas of life. It leads to long life.

Proverbs 3: 16 Length of days is in her right hand,
and in her left hand riches and honor.
17 Her ways are ways of pleasantness,

God promises long life to those who honour their parents in one of the commandments. That means that it is so important that God chose it as a commandment. It is the only commandment that has a direct promise linked to it. These were the commandments that God wrote with His own finger on the tablets of stone and gave to Moses.

Exodus 20: 12 Honor your father and your mother, that your days may be long in the land which the Lord your God is giving you.
Life and Death

Obeying commands of God prolongs your life. Promised through Moses for the children of Abraham, who became Israel, God promises the blessings of choosing to live for God, obeying His commandments or the curses of the law for disobeying God. God gives people free will to choose His way or to go their own way, which is the sin of choosing against God – rebellion and pride – the same sins of Satan. The blessings of God include total and complete blessings discussed throughout the book of Deuteronomy. It includes, health, prosperity, finances and abundance, blessings on children, animals, and all within one's sphere of influence. The blessing is not simply long life but joyful, abundant life that encompasses all aspects of a human's life.

Deuteronomy 11: 8 Therefore you must keep all the commandments which

I am commanding you today, so that you may be strong and go in and possess the land which you are going to possess; 9 and that you may prolong your days in the land which the Lord swore to your fathers to give to them and to their descendants, a land flowing with milk and honey.

Clearly God is saying that obedience to the commandments prolongs your life and makes one strong. The blessings of the land of milk and honey seem hard for the modern-day person to understand. The blessings of the promised land to Abraham, Moses and Joshua is a gift especially to Israel. Please see that also God has a promise for each of us. God has a place of blessing for us to inherit and live in. Israel began to be agricultural after they inherited the promised land.

The blessings of "milk" can be seen as there being lush green pastures for their herds of cows, sheep, goats etc. To us it would mean the healthiest fruitful atmosphere to live in. The blessings of "honey" would mean there would be beauty in the land such as flowers and shrubs and flowering trees bring so that bees may thrive. A long life surrounded by beauty and lush vegetation is the dream of any farmer.

Blessing or curse

We choose to obey God and live in the blessing or disobey God and receive the results of the curse. God gives us the choice. We do not have to choose Him. It would be foolish not to choose Him. That is why it is essential that we teach the things of God to our children and to those who don't know God. If they were to know how good God is and to experience the favour and blessing of living in communion with God, they would not want to go any other way.

Deuteronomy 11: 26 See, I am setting before you today a blessing and a curse: 27 the blessing if you obey the commandments of the Lord your God, which I am commanding you today, 28 and the curse, if you will not obey the commandments of the Lord your God, but turn from the way which I am commanding you today, to go after other gods which you have not known.

The curses listed in Deuteronomy are long and horrible. Just as the blessings offer abundance and joy, the curses describe poverty, sickness, disease and horrible life conditions. Those things outside the blessings of God are consequences of disobedience. They are the result of the curse upon Adam and Eve. Disobeying God's commandments is a step into the realm of sin and the consequences of it.

There is nothing worth losing your relationship with God. Nothing or no one is worth sacrificing your soul (Matthew 16: 26).

Sin separates you from God

If there is sin against God or turning away from God to sin – Repent immediately. If you know it is wrong, thank God – it means you have a conscience. Don't ignore it. God is merciful. Jesus who saved you, will forgive you. The blood of Jesus applies to you if you will repent. That means to turn away from sin, towards God. It means to confess that you have sinned and you humbly ask Jesus to cleanse you with His blood. Truly, Jesus will forgive you, if you will turn towards God, God will cleanse you and renew you and give you renewed friendship and communion with Him. You do not need to get saved all over again. You do need to repent though. It can be a moment so brief that only God and you know about it. Repentance is an attitude of the heart. It is a deliberate turning away from what you know is wrong and turning to God.

1 John 1: 9 If we confess our sins, He is faithful and just to forgive us our sins and cleanse us from all unrighteousness.

1 John 2: 2 My little children, I am writing these things to you, so that you do not sin. But if anyone does sin, we have an Advocate with the Father, Jesus Christ the Righteous One. 2 He is the atoning sacrifice for our sins, and not for ours only, but also for the sins of the whole world.

Consequences for unrepentant sin

There are consequences for sin. It is the curse of Adam. It is death. The same death spoken of in Genesis – that if you take that which is forbidden you shall surely die. Death is first spiritual – separation from God; results will be in your human body as well as in all spheres of your influence. The person will lose communion with God, lose the favour of God and be living against God.

Romans 6: 23 For the wages of sin is death, but the gift of God is eternal life through Jesus Christ our Lord.

It is possible for someone who has known God and lived in the blessings to disobey God and go a different way – a sinful disobedient way. God never forces us. No matter what should happen to you, believe the truth that Jesus died for your sins. Jesus is merciful. He will forgive you.

Turn towards God – even if it is hard – God is the way to a prosperous, healthy, long life of joy and all the blessings He has promised – as well as eternal life. I have not emphasized the eternal life part because most Christians believe that Jesus is eternal life. Some Christians do not know that Jesus wants to prosperous in our present life also.

Good news of Jesus – bringing cleansing from sin and healing

1 John 1: 9 If we confess our sins, He is faithful and just to forgive us our sins and cleanse us from all unrighteousness.

It is essential that you know you are forgiven. God's word promises that if you confess your sin, to God, you will be forgiven. You either know it because you completely believe the Word of God or you don't. You must believe what the scripture says. If you truly repent, He truly washes the sin away as though it never existed. Whether or not you "feel" forgiven is up to you. You, your spirit must come into agreement with God's Word and believe because God said it and God always speaks the truth. Receive your forgiveness by thanking God out loud. Say " Thank you God for forgiving me and washing my sin as though it never existed. Help to live uprightly and to never do it again." It may be important for your spirit to hear your own mouth saying those words.

Return to God means God will once more bless you.

As soon as you repent, you are forgiven. You get up and strengthen your faith and start living for God. Sometimes, you need someone to be accountable to if it is a habitual sin or bad habit or addiction. You may need a mature Christian to pray with you for deliverance. The good news is there is no sin that cannot be forgiven. There is no sin that can keep you in addiction or bondage. Jesus Christ conquered all sin and addiction. Jesus Christ can set you free (John 8: 36).

If it something that causes guilt, know it is not God that is giving you that feeling. If you repent, the sin is gone. You could get some wine or juice and some bread and literally offer yourself as a living willing sacrifice to God. You rededicate your life to God and take the communion which are symbols of our blood covenant with Jesus Christ. It is an excellent way to show God you mean to live holy.

God's Blessings

God's blessings cover all aspects of our lives. Living with God means relationship. It is not religion. Religion is a list of things you can do or can't do. True faith in Jesus is desiring to live in God's presence experiencing the joy of His friendship. The Holy Spirit within you prompting you and leading you throughout your life. You will know joy and pleasure beyond what any person can describe because of God's Spirit living on the inside of you. You will be blessed in all your ways. Blessing means special favour or fruitfulness – like a tree bearing much fruit – a full ripe lush life.

The blessing is God's special favour on every part of your life. It includes your career, your family, your animals, your fields (whether they be agricultural or economic). Please see literally God delights in blessings us. The scripture literally says " God will again rejoice over you for good." God rejoices in our pleasure. If it is hard for you to accept, think of the special love of a parent with a child and how that parent delights in seeing that child happy and joyful. Parents who love their children often buy them things that make them rejoice. They give them special things they might not give to anyone else. It is that same kind of parental love God feels towards us.

Deuteronomy 30: 9 The Lord your God will make you prosper in every work of your hand, in the offspring of your body, and in the offspring of your livestock, and in the produce of your land, for good. For the Lord will once again rejoice over you for good, just as He rejoiced over your fathers,
10 if you obey the voice of the Lord your God, by keeping His commandments and His statutes which are written in this Book of the Law, and if you return to the Lord your God with all your heart and with all your soul.

Living with God, means living wholly for Him. It might mean that repentance is necessary very often. For example, I was not raised in a Christian home. I did not know God's Word. I did not know God's ways. The first several years of my Christian life I went to every altar call praying over myself, sometimes others praying for me. I realized that I was not living according to God's Word in many aspects of my life. I would pray "God help me to love what you love and hate what you hate." That type of prayer will get God helping you overcome any habit or sin. The Holy Spirit can enlighten you and show you a different way. I mean it is as simple as God showing you a different way.

For instance, I would often drive to my friend's church. The way I knew was going through several main freeways. One day my friend explained to me there was a shorter and easier way. Once I receive it and tried it, I realized it was truly the best way. It changed my life. God can reveal His ways to you and you can see His ways as being the best ways. It starts with a willing decision to turn to God.

Living in the blessing

I describe someone living in covenant with God as someone who has a special protection (Psalm 5: 12). God is a shield around your life protecting you. If you step outside of God's will, you step outside of God's blessing. Outside of God's will, things are under the curse of the sin of Adam. Life is hard and there are many results of the curse of those who willfully disobey God's commandments. That is why it is essential that if you sin, you immediately repent. Turn to God and accept the blood of Jesus as washing you and cleansing you. Pray it. Confess it and live in abundance.

Jesus Christ lived imparting salvation, healing and deliverance to those around him. The scripture says He was doing good. Part of what He was doing was healing people who were oppressed by the devil. That is a clear indication that God does not place sickness upon a person. God would never go against Himself. Sickness is part of the curse of Adam. Sickness is part of the curse of the law. God want you to be whole, to be healed to be healthy. Knowing it is the first step in receiving it.

Acts 10: 38 how God anointed Jesus of Nazareth with the Holy Spirit and with power, who went about doing good and healing all who were oppressed by the devil, for God was with Him.

3 GOD'S WILL TO HEAL PEOPLE

CHAPTER 3
Examples of God's Healing Mercies

God expressed His will to heal people throughout the scriptures. It is part of the inheritance of the blessing of the LORD. Jesus often healed people or did miracles because he was moved with compassion. His delight to give us health, long life and prosperity is recorded throughout the scriptures.

Psalm 103 – Reasons to praise God

One of my favourite Psalms is Psalm 103 because it covers so many aspects of God's mercy towards us. It begins with praises giving glory to God. Thanksgiving is given by expressing the excellent aspects God has shown to the psalm writer. First, there is blessing because He is God. There is no one else like him.

Next, there is praise given because of the benefits or blessings of serving God. The psalm writer says – forget not his benefits which means he is keeping them in his remembrance, the good things God has done for him.

There is forgiveness for all iniquity or inherited sin, including the sin of Adam. Any sins passed on from ancestors who did not repent, can be forgiven. There is thanksgiving for healing of all diseases. Clearly God the healer is given praise. Redeeming your life from the pit certainly means saves you or redeems you so you do not end up with the unrighteous who die. It also means though any situation that can be negative. Not only does God do these things but He crowns you with lovingkindness and tender mercies.

Literally God's mercy and compassion towards you comes in overwhelming waves of glory. If you know God, you can confirm truly His mercies are overwhelming. The passion and zeal that He expresses towards us is overwhelming. He loves us so completely and His desire towards us is only good. He delights in prospering us. He renews our strength. It is of God's mercy that we receive these benefits.

Divine Healing is God's will

Benefits are forgiveness, healing and blessing and salvation

Psalm 103: 1 Bless the Lord, O my soul,
and all that is within me, bless His holy name.
2 Bless the Lord, O my soul,
and forget not all His benefits,
3 who forgives all your iniquities,
who heals all your diseases,
4 who redeems your life from the pit,
who crowns you with lovingkindness and tender mercies,
5 who satisfies your mouth with good things,
so that your youth is renewed like the eagle's.

There are conditions of covenant life with God. Once more examining the scriptures that discuss blessings and curses in Deuteronomy show us that it is our choice. We can choose God's way the way of the blessing or we can disobey God and live in the curse because of Adam's sin. God gives it to us plainly. It is not a deep secret or hard to understand thing. God is simple. He gives us a choice. He makes clear the consequences of the choices. He honours our free will to choose.

Deuteronomy 11: 26 See, I am setting before you today a blessing and a curse: 27 the blessing if you obey the commandments of the Lord your God, which I am commanding you today, 28 and the curse, if you will not obey the commandments of the Lord your God, but turn from the way which I am commanding you today, to go after other gods which you have not known

Sickness is part of the curse. If you do not choose God, the curses will come upon you.. The place of protection is the place of blessing; it is following the commandments of God. Obeying and living for God brings us abundant life. Living outside the umbrella of protection we live in the curse of Adam's sin. I have only included one scripture from Deuteronomy on the curse. Moses copied all that God spoke to Him and He read them to all the congregation of Israel. Later, Joshua also read them to all of Israel. These things were taught and passed on so that people would know how to please God and how to repent if they sinned. Someone who willfully sins, lives outside the protection and blessing of God.

Deuteronomy 28: 58 If you are not careful to observe all the words of this law that are written in this book so that you may fear this glorious and fearful name, the Lord your God, 59 then the Lord will bring extraordinary plagues on you and your descendants, even great long-lasting plagues, and severe and long-lasting sicknesses. 60 Moreover, He will bring all the diseases of Egypt upon you, which you were afraid of, and they will cling to you. 61 Also every sickness and every plague which is not written in the Book of the Law will the Lord bring upon you until you are destroyed.

The Messiah

The Messiah mentioned first in Genesis 3 as the offspring of the woman who would be the Saviour to cleanse them from Adam's sin is mentioned throughout the Old Testament. Jesus Christ fulfilled each of the Messianic prophecies as He lived on earth and in his death, burial and resurrection. Jesus the healer is mentioned in the prophecies also.

Jesus would bring wholeness shalom peace – wholeness – to spirit soul and body. Isaiah 53 is a usual scripture people use to preach that Jesus is the Messiah because he fulfilled all of these things. Please note especially in verse 4 that He "carried our sorrows", meaning that we do not have to grieve as others grieve. Jesus paid the price for our liberty.

Isaiah 53: 1Who has believed our report?
   And to whom has the arm of the Lord been revealed?
2 For he grew up before Him as a tender plant
   and as a root out of a dry ground.
He has no form or majesty that we should look upon him
   nor appearance that we should desire him.
3 He was despised and rejected of men,
   a man of sorrows and acquainted with grief.
And we hid, as it were, our faces from him;
   he was despised, and we did not esteem him.

He was wounded for our transgressions means He took our place, dying for our sins, giving us salvation. Also, He was bruised and beaten for our iniquities. He paid the penalty for the sin of Adam and any family inequities. He suffered that we might experience His eternal peace. Because He was beaten and whipped, literally we can be healing. He took upon Himself all sickness and disease. Jesus experienced these things not only proving He was Messiah but also showing to us it is His will to heal us. He died on the cross so that we could receive the blessings of the Mosaic covenant of health and long life.

Isaiah 53: 4 Surely he has borne our grief
and carried our sorrows;
Yet we esteemed him stricken,
smitten of God, and afflicted.
5 But he was wounded for our transgressions,
he was bruised for our iniquities;
the chastisement of our peace was upon him,
and by his stripes we are healed.
6 All of us like sheep have gone astray;
each of us has turned to his own way,
but the Lord has laid on him
the iniquity of us all.

Jesus the Messiah Reveals Himself

Jesus read Isiah 61 in the synagogue as He revealed Himself. After reading these verses He spoke saying,
Luke 4: 21 And He began to say to them, "Today this Scripture is fulfilled in your hearing."

He announced that Messiah had come. The reaction of the people was to want to kill him. No one expected Messiah to come being born of a woman. Possibly, they expected Jesus riding on a white horse with crowns on his head much like He will in his soon coming kingdom.

That day in the synagogue, Jesus announced the good news that Israel had been expecting for thousands of years. The gospel or good news is that Messiah has come. He has fulfilled all prophecy. No longer are people cut off from God. No longer do people have to be slaves to sin. There is good news. Jesus is the healer. No longer do people have to suffer. If they will believe on the LORD Jesus Christ, they will be healed. The type of healing I am describing is wholeness. It is complete prosperity: soul, spirit and body.

The good news Jesus announced included these things:

Deliverance from curse of law
Prosperity
Healing
Abundance
Liberty

Joy

The acceptable year of the LORD – the day of salvation had come.

In practical ways it literally means poor people do not have to remain poor. God has made a way to end the curse of poverty. It means God can heal the inner man or soul of a person. To someone who does not know God it means God is giving opportunities to know God. There is comfort for those who grieve. God can give a person joy instead of grief, praise instead of sorrow. Jesus is the Saviour wholly. Just as the curse of Adam's sin affected all aspects of man's life, the blessings of covenant with Jesus cover all aspects of human life.

Isaiah 61: 1 The Spirit of the Lord God is upon me
because the Lord has anointed me
to preach good news to the poor;
He has sent me to heal the broken-hearted,
to proclaim liberty to the captives,
and the opening of the prison to those who are bound;
2 to proclaim the acceptable year of the Lord
and the day of vengeance of our God;
to comfort all who mourn,
3 to preserve those who mourn in Zion,
to give to them beauty
for ashes,
the oil of joy
for mourning,
the garment of praise
for the spirit of heaviness,
that they might be called trees of righteousness,
the planting of the Lord,
that He might be glorified.

Although these covenant blessings are given to all who believe in Jesus, many people do not know the truth of them. What it means is that they do not receive it because they don't even know about it. That is my motive for writing this book. If you know the blessings of the covenant, you can receive them. I would compare it to a huge store that is giving free samples of something. All the people who passed that place received a free sample. Those who did not pass that way, didn't even know what was being given away free. They don't even know what they are missing.

Healing of Naaman the leper

Faith for healing can come to non-believers who are need of healing or a miracle.

Naaman the Leper

The Arameans were fighting against Israel and taking captives as slaves. They were clearly the enemy, yet one unnamed Israelite girl who was taken as a slave was moved with compassion towards her master. It is somewhat amazing to realize that the girl was taken out of her home, out of her country and made to be a slave, yet she cared about her master who had leprosy. She knew God. She knew the prophets of God. She mentions it to the wife of Naaman. By her words and sincerity, the wife of Naaman knew it must be true. There was no logical motive for the girl to mention it if she were not sincere. Because of it, Naaman's wife convinces Naaman to return to Israel and to go to the king to inquire about the prophet of God who can heal.

This is a miracle happening. An invader of Israel and enemy of Israel, humbles himself to go and ask for healing. He doesn't know where the prophet is – so he goes to the king of Israel. Please know, I am sure this was not his first attempt to be healed. For him to do such a thing, he most likely had tried everything he could in his own country. His god did not heal him. He must have wanted out of his sickness so much that it made him ride the distance and humble himself. Because he is an influential person, and because he has authority, there is some pride in him. He goes to Israel. 2 Kings 5: 2 The Arameans had gone out raiding and had taken captive a little girl from the land of Israel, and she waited on the wife of Naaman. 3 She said to her mistress, "If only my lord were before the prophet who is in Samaria! Then he would take away his leprosy from him."

As Naaman speaks with the king of Israel (not following God) the king tears his clothes. This means a deep grief. He is admitting he can do nothing. I don't know if he thought it was a way to attack Israel more or if he simply had no faith in God. Elisha the prophet gets the news and invites Naaman to come to him to show that the God of Israel is mighty. What is going on is a desire for healing but please see how there is an authority issue going on. The girl has faith to impart to her mistress and her master. The enemy or conqueror, Naaman, goes to the king he has conquered requesting healing. The king of Israel does not know God or believe in healing. Elisha the prophet is used by God to show the power of God not only to Naaman but also so that all people will know God is a healer.

I believe Naaman had some pride in him, maybe because he was the conqueror, or maybe because the king didn't even know about God the healer. He goes to the prophet, but Elisha does not even come out of his home. He sends a messenger to tell Naaman what to do to be healed. The message is simple. It's almost ridiculous. He is instructed to bath in the Jordan river dunking seven occasions under the water.

2 Kings 5: 8 But when Elisha the man of God heard that the king of Israel had torn his clothes, he sent word to the king, saying, "Why have you torn your clothes? Let him come to me, and he will know that there is a prophet in Israel." 9 So Naaman came with his horses and chariot and stood at the entrance to the house of Elisha. 10 Elisha sent a messenger to him, saying, "Go and wash seven times in the Jordan, and your flesh will be returned and cleansed."

The instruction coming from a servant of Elisha, not even Elisha's own mouth must have seemed insulting to him. Naaman doesn't want to obey the instruction. Perhaps he thought none of it was true. He doubted it and says he would rather bathe in his own river in his own country. He would not have obeyed the simple instruction.

2 Kings 5: 11 But Naaman became angry and went away and said to himself, "Surely he could have come out, and stood and called on the name of the Lord his God, and waved his hand over the infected area, and taken away the leprosy. 12 Are not Abana and Pharpar, rivers of Damascus, better than all the waters of Israel? Could I not wash in them and be clean?" So he turned and went away in a rage.

Once more God shows how servants can influence their masters as his servants speak to him with mercy and logic. They encourage him to try it even if it is simple. They persuade him to obey with their soft, kind words appealing to his logic. Naaman is influenced. He dunks under the Jordan river. Upon rising from the river at the last dunk, his skin is completely healed. He no longer had leprosy. He is completely healed. What he does is return to thank the prophet of God Elisha and to offer gifts to him for his healing. Elisha accepts no gifts. Naaman becomes a believer in the God if Israel.

2 Kings 5: 13 But his servants approached and spoke to him, "My father, if the prophet had told you to do some great thing, would you not have done it? How much more when he said to you, 'Wash and be clean'?" 14 So he went down and dipped himself in the Jordan seven times, according to the

word of the man of God, and his flesh returned like the flesh of a little boy, and he was clean.

Healing of King Hezekiah

The King of Israel was known as a good king. He served God. He grew ill and near death. A prophet of God announces to him to prepare to die. I'm sure no one wants to hear such unpleasant news. Hezekiah earnestly weeps and prays asking God to live. He reminds God that he has served God faithfully. He loved his life and wanted more of it. He went to God as the source. He did these things correctly. Because of his humility and his prayers, God has mercy on him and extends his life.

2 Kings 20: 1 In those days Hezekiah became ill and was near death. The prophet Isaiah son of Amoz came to him, and said to him, "Thus says the Lord: Set your house in order, for you shall die and not live."

2 Then he turned his face toward the wall and prayed to the Lord, saying, 3 "Please, O Lord, remember how I have walked before You faithfully and with an undivided heart and have done what is good in Your sight." And Hezekiah wept bitterly.

The prophet of God is stopped by God and sent to return to the king with a new message. He gives specific instruction on what to do to receive healing. His life is extended 15 years. The compassion of God hearing and answering the prayer of one of his servants is shown. Much can occur in 15 years. Hezekiah recovers. A simple, true prayer acknowledging God brings a healing and longer life to him.

2 Kings 20: 4 Now before Isaiah had come out of the middle courtyard, the word of the Lord came to him, saying, 5 "Turn back and say to Hezekiah the leader of My people: Thus says the Lord, the God of David your father: I have heard your prayer; I have seen your tears. I will heal you. On the third day, you shall go up to the house of the Lord. 6 I will add to your days fifteen years, and I will deliver you and this city from the hand of the king of Assyria. I will defend this city for My own sake and for the sake of David My servant."

2 Kings 20: 7 Then Isaiah said, "Take a cake of figs." So they took it and laid it on the boil, and he recovered.

Healing of Shunamite woman's son – resurrection from the dead

Elisha is known as the prophet who washed the hands of Elijah. What it means is that he served Elijah from the moment Elijah chose him. He also did twice as many miracles as Elijah. He was known for a double portion anointing on his life. There was a woman who was kind to Elisha and her son died. She shuts the door on him, takes her donkey and rides out to meet Elisha. She does not give any negative confession. No words of unbelief come out of her mouth. Rather than tell her husband their son died, she goes to the prophet believing that God can use him to do a miracle. Elisha tells his servant to go heal her son. The woman will not depart from Elisha and begs him to come with her. She knows he is a prophet of God and believes God can use him. She also believes it is necessary for him to come in person. Elisha goes. Elisha sees the boy has died. He prays to God asking for a miracle. He lays on the child and life is restored to the boy. God raised the dead through the prophet Elisha.

2 Kings 4: 32 When Elisha came into the house, he saw that the boy was dead, lying on his bed. 33 So he went in, and shut the door on the two of them, and prayed to the Lord. 34 He went up and lay on the child, put his face on his face, and his eyes on his eyes, and his hands on his hands. Then he bent over the child, and the child's flesh warmed. 35 Then he got down, walked once back and forth in the house, and went up, and bent over him; the boy sneezed seven times, and the boy opened his eyes.

36 Then Elisha called Gehazi and said, "Call the Shunammite woman." So he called her, and she came to him. Then he said, "Pick up your son." 37 Then she came in, fell at his feet, and bowed down to the ground. Then she picked up her son and went out.

Sometimes someone with a known gift of healing or anointing for healings or miracles is used by God. I have been in large meetings of 20, 000 people who are gathering to praise God with the hope of being healed because of the anointing on the preacher. I myself attended this type of conference, standing in proxy for a friend who needed a miracle healing from cancer. I not only believed in the sure gift of anointing on the minister of God, but I believed that God would honour my faith as I stood there for a friend.

If you are ill, and you know of a minister who comes to your area who has the gifts of healing and miracles, get into the meeting if at all possible. I have seen people wheeled in wheel chairs and some on beds with wheels. They did not leave the same way they came in. They were healed. People who are desperate for healing will come to people who they know has healing gifts. All believers can pray for the sick that they be healed, but some people have special anointing of them for healing and miracles.

Get Prayer Support

In a different instance, my own mother's near death, I prayed. I got people to pray. I sent prayer requests and donations to ministries I know believe in healing and teach and preach healing with signs and wonders following. That means people get healed because of the ministry. You do not have to give an offering to receive healing. I did it showing my faith towards God and also to support those ministries thanking God for them.

All the ministries I support pray for their partners and those who write requesting prayer. I was strengthened knowing that I had sent to those who would faithfully pray. The Christian ministers I support are especially important to me because I was the first Christian in my family. I did not have a large base of support in my home. My church prayed; my friends prayed. What you don't want when you need a miracle, is someone uttering an unscriptural prayer or words of unbelief. I am choosey about who I request prayer from.

I mention my brief testimony here so that you may also write prayer requests to reputable minsters who believe in healing and who pray for those who write to them. The body of Christ is more than just your local church. If you know someone has a healing gift, and can't get into a meeting, write and request prayer. Some ministries will send a prayer cloth.

Prayer Cloths

Acts 19: 11 God worked powerful miracles by the hands of Paul. 12 So handkerchiefs or aprons he had touched were brought to the sick, and the diseases left them, and the evil spirits went out of them.

A prayer cloth is exactly as it says. It is a piece of cloth that people have prayed over in faith for healing to be imparted. There is no magic; it isn't the cloth itself. What occurs is the faith of the people praying imparts spiritual substance for healing into the fibers of the cloth. The person receiving the prayer cloth, believes and receives the healing in agreement.

My mum pinned her prayer cloths to the inside of her gown. She knew people had prayed. I also prayed for her with the cloth. I prayed with her receiving the healing by Jesus Christ in agreement with the ministers who prayed over the prayer cloths. She kept it as a reminder that she was not alone. There were Christians praying and believing for her healing.

4 JESUS HEALED

Jesus Christ healed
Chapter 3

Healing of noble man's son

Jesus in ministry began by announcing that he was Messiah. He also began demonstrating it. He not only had the healing gifts but he also spoke with authority. In the instance of the nobleman's son – he simply spoke the word and it occurred at the instance that he spoke it.

Only God has the authority to create with words. It was God's word that created all things. God spoke them into being. The same authority to speak creative life-giving words was upon Jesus. Jesus gave his disciples the same authority. The same authority is given to us as believers in Jesus Christ.

Matthew 28: 18 Then Jesus came and spoke to them, saying, "All authority has been given to Me in heaven and on earth. 19 Go therefore and make disciples of all nations, baptizing them in the name of the Father and of the Son and of the Holy Spirit, 20 teaching them to observe all things I have commanded you. And remember, I am with you always, even to the end of the age." Amen.

John 4: 43 After the two days He departed from there and went to Galilee. 44 For Jesus Himself testified that a prophet has no honor in his own country. 45 Then, when He came to Galilee, the Galileans welcomed Him, having seen all the things He did at Jerusalem at the feast. For they had also gone to the feast.

46 So Jesus came again to Cana of Galilee where He had made the water wine. And there was a certain nobleman whose son was sick in Capernaum. 47 When he heard that Jesus had come out of Judea into Galilee, he went to Him, pleading that He would come down and heal his son, for he was at the point of death.

48 Then Jesus said to him, "Unless you see signs and wonders, you will not believe."

49 The nobleman said to Him, "Sir, come down before my child dies."

50 Jesus said to him, "Go your way. Your son lives."

And the man believed the word that Jesus spoke to him, and he went his way. 51 While he was going down, his servants met him and told him, "Your son lives!" 52 When he inquired of them the hour when he began to heal, they answered, "Yesterday at the seventh hour the fever left him."

53 Then the father knew that it was at the same hour in which Jesus said to him, "Your son lives." So he and his whole household believed.

It is important to know that words release life or death. It is possible to send a word of healing as Jesus did. Secondly, it is important to note that the nobleman believed Jesus. His faith was strong enough to believe that if Jesus said it, it would occur. As he went, he received word that his healing occurred exactly after Jesus spoke it.

Although sometimes healing occurs with laying on of hands and impartation, sometimes healing comes by sending a word. A word spoken with faith pierces though the spirit realm directly to its target. It isn't always that way. God chooses different ways to heal people. That is why it is called gifts of healing. There is more than one manifestation of healing. I say this to encourage you; should a minister anointed with the Holy Spirit not be able to come to your territory, but you send a prayer request, it is possible that as the people pray over the requests, healing can be sent by word of faith.

Testimonies of healing can lead others to Christ

The was a place of healing at Bethesda. It was known that an angel would come and stir the waters and the first person who got into the pool was healed. Many people gathered there. I don't understand the statement but I know it is possible. Throughout history there have been special places where healings and miracles occur. Usually, people build a shrine or a temple there. The point is, God was already healing people at that place. Jesus came there and saw a paralyzed man who could not get into the water although he was at that place for many years. Jesus asks him if he wants to be healed. It seems odd. Jesus should have known that a person at that place wanted to be healed. Jesus was getting the man to examine his own heart. Jesus commanded him and the man obeyed the voice of authority. As he obeyed Jesus, he was completely healed.

Jesus commands him to get up and walk.

John 5: 5 After this there was a feast of the Jews, and Jesus went up to Jerusalem. 2 Now in Jerusalem by the Sheep Gate there is a pool, which in Hebrew is called Bethesda, having five porches. 3 In these lay a great crowd of invalids, blind, lame, and paralyzed, waiting for the moving of the water. 4 For an angel went down at a certain time into the pool and stirred up the water. After the stirring of the water, whoever stepped in first was healed of whatever disease he had. 5 A certain man was there who had an illness for thirty-eight years. 6 When Jesus saw him lying there, and knew that he had been in that condition now a long time, He said to him, "Do you want to be healed?"

7 The sick man answered Him, "Sir, I have no one to put me into the pool when the water is stirred. But while I am coming, another steps down before me."

8 Jesus said to him, "Rise, take up your bed and walk." 9 Immediately the man was healed, took up his bed, and walked.

Healing of Blind Man

In a different type of healing, a creative miracle, Jesus did a strange thing. First, he proved to his disciples that sin was not the cause of the disease. Many people had interpreted the promises of the blessings in the law believing that only sinners were sick or ill. Most people who kept the commandments were healthy. Jesus corrects them by saying that neither the man nor his parents sinned. He turns the statement around completely saying that it was so that God could be glorified.

Jesus had the man brought to him and spit in the clay and made mud and placed it on the man's eyes. This bizarre sort of way of healing showed several things. First, the same Jesus who was there with God creating Adam from the clay, was bringing healing to the man. Also, he was demonstrating the gift of working of miracles. There is a part of the working of miracles that always requires faith to do something. He commanded the man to go wash his eyes in the pool of Siloam. As the man obeyed, he was completely healed. The disciples saw a creative miracle. Someone born blind was given seeing eyes. It brought glory to God. The man's life was completely transformed. No longer was he unable to work. He could earn a living. He had been given a new chance at life.

John 9: 9 As Jesus passed by, He saw a man blind from birth. 2 His disciples asked Him, "Rabbi, who sinned, this man or his parents, that he was born blind?"

3 Jesus answered, "Neither this man nor his parents sinned. But it happened so that the works of God might be displayed in him. 4 I must do the works of Him who sent Me while it is day. Night is coming when no one can work. 5 While I am in the world, I am the light of the world."

6 When He had said this, He spat on the ground and made clay with the saliva. He anointed the eyes of the blind man with the clay, 7 and said to him, "Go, wash in the pool of Siloam" (which means "Sent"). So he went away and washed, and returned seeing.

Resurrection of Lazarus

A week before his own death, burial and resurrection, Jesus hears of his friend Lazarus being ill near unto death. He waits and continues in the place he was at even though he loved Lazarus and his family. He later goes to Lazarus home but Martha and Mary are weeping because Lazarus is dead and buried. Both of them, respond to Jesus wondering why he did not come earlier. They knew he could have healed him. Jesus wanted to show more than healing with the case of Lazarus.

Jesus is life.

Jesus is the way the truth the life (John 14: 6).

Jesus raises the dead because He is life. He doesn't say he has life; he says he is the resurrection and the life. Only God could say He is life. Only God can create life. Jesus assures Martha that her brother will be resurrected. She acknowledges it believing in the resurrection day. Jesus reveals to her, to Mary, to all those who are gathered that He is resurrection life.

John 11: 23 Jesus said to her, "Your brother will rise again."

24 Martha said to Him, "I know that he will rise again in the resurrection on the last day."

25 Jesus said to her, "I am the resurrection and the life. He who believes in Me, though he may die, yet shall he live. 26 And whoever lives and believes in Me shall never die. Do you believe this?"

27 She said to Him, "Yes, Lord, I believe that You are the Christ, the Son of God, who is to come into the world."

Jesus goes to the tomb of Lazarus. They try to reason with Jesus that Lazarus has been dead for more than 3 days. Jesus commands Lazarus to come out of death, out of the tomb. Lazarus, spirit obeys the creator and comes out of the tomb. All that saw it knew a miracle had taken place. Mary and Martha realize that Jesus is more than a healer. Resurrection life brings a new chance at life for Lazarus.

John 11: 43 When He had said this, He cried out with a loud voice, "Lazarus, come out!" 44 He who was dead came out, his hands and feet wrapped with grave clothes, and his face wrapped with a cloth.

Jesus said to them, "Unbind him, and let him go."

Healing can come different ways

Healing can come in manifold ways. It can occur in a prayer of agreement. Jesus promised us that if 2 or 3 of us got together and prayed, we would receive our answer. That is why it is essential that you have someone to pray in agreement with. If there isn't a family member or friend, don't forget to contact the healing ministries. A prayer with real faith is much stronger than any type of unbelieving prayer. The key word is agreement. You and the person or persons praying should agree on the matter.

Prayer of agreement

The person must believe that Jesus is the healer. If someone doesn't know if God wants to heal or not, you don't agree in faith with doubters. You cannot come into agreement with just anyone. Your faith must be the same.

Matthew 18: 19 "Again I say to you, that if two of you agree on earth about anything they ask, it will be done for them by My Father who is in heaven. 20 For where two or three are assembled in My name, there I am in their midst."

Anointing with oil

Oil was used throughout the Bible to show different things. It is symbolic of God's Holy Spirit. God instructed Moses to create a Holy

Anointing oil; there was a specific recipe given. Only the priests were permitted to make it. Only the priests were permitted to use it. It was only to be used in the duties as a priest. (Exodus 30: 22-33)

Oil was used by Samuel to anoint Saul as King of Israel. He also poured a horn of oil over David to anoint him as king. (1 Samuel 9 – 10) (1 Samuel 16: 1 – 13)

In the New Testament, the prayer of faith with anointing of oil is used to heal. Both the prayer of faith and the anointing of oil go together. Faith is necessary in the prayer. The oil is only representative of the Holy Spirit. Together as elders or ministers pray the prayer of faith over a person, not only will the person be healed but his or her sins may be forgiven.

James 5: 13 Is anyone among you suffering? Let him pray. Is anyone merry? Let him sing psalms. 14 Is anyone sick among you? Let him call for the elders of the church, and let them pray over him, anointing him with oil in the name of the Lord. 15 And the prayer of faith will save the sick, and the Lord will raise him up. And if he has committed any sins, he will be forgiven. 16 Confess your faults to one another and pray for one another, that you may be healed. The effective, fervent prayer of a righteous man accomplishes much.

The healing faith of friends – also forgiveness of sins

In a different instance, Jesus is preaching in a home where many people have gathered. Some friends of a paralyzed man wanted to get their friend to Jesus so he could be healed. He was carried on a mat. They couldn't get anywhere near Jesus because of the crowd so they with faith, climbed onto the roof with their friend and lowered him from the roof in front of Jesus. It does not say the paralyzed man had faith. The scriptures does give credit to the friends for having faith. They believed Jesus could and would heal their friend if they could only get to Jesus.

Healing of paralyzed man

Jesus sees more than the man's physical body. In this instance, there was some sin that had to be forgiven. He demonstrates his authority to heal the paralyzed man but also his authority to forgive sins. Many people there believed he was blaspheming by saying he could forgive sins. Jesus forgives the man's sins by stating it. This must have ignited faith in the man. Only he and God knew about any sin he had.

Mark 2 2 Again, He entered Capernaum after some days. And it was reported that He was in the house. 2 Immediately many were gathered together, so that there was no room to receive them, not even at the door. And He preached the word to them. 3 They came to Him bringing one sick with paralysis, who was carried by four men. 4 When they could not come near Him due to the crowding, they uncovered the roof where He was. When they had broken it open, they let down the bed on which the paralytic lay. 5 When Jesus saw their faith, He said to the paralytic, "Son, your sins are forgiven you."

6 But some of the scribes were sitting there, reasoning in their hearts, 7 "Why does this Man speak such blasphemies? Who can forgive sins but God alone?"

Jesus sees the unbelief in the crowd of people and mentions that healing someone's sins is not harder than healing a person. The truth was none of them could do either. Jesus spoke to the man commanding him to get up. The man obeyed. This showed not only the power to heal but the power to forgive sins.

Mark 2: 8 Immediately, when Jesus perceived in His spirit that they so reasoned within themselves, He said to them, "Why do you contemplate these things in your hearts? 9 Which is easier to say to the paralytic: 'Your sins are forgiven you,' or to say, 'Rise, take up your bed and walk'? 10 But that you may know that the Son of Man has authority on earth to forgive sins," He said to the paralytic, 11 "I say to you, rise, and take up your bed, and go your way to your house." 12 Immediately he rose, picked up the bed, and went out in front of them all, so that they were all amazed and glorified God, saying, "We never saw anything like this!"

Faith for healing

There is a type of healing that can come to person who truly believes he or she will be healed. For instance, the woman with the issue of blood (hemorrhaging) for all of those years desired to be healed and tried almost everything. She spent all her money on searching for a cure but finally, Jesus was passing by. She believed within herself that if she could just touch the hem of his garment, she could be healed. Her faith was fixed on Jesus and getting near to him.

She had faith in a touch of Jesus bringing healing, She pressed through a crowd of people and reached out and touched the hem of his garment; immediately she was healed. She did not even speak with Jesus. He did not even pray for her. She within her own self believed. Jesus felt the touch of faith. Even though there were throngs of people every place around him, all sorts of people brushing against him or touching him, he felt a touch of faith. Her faith brought healing to her. It stopped Jesus and wanted to know who touched him. She admitted the truth. Jesus said her faith had made her whole. I would term this type of faith to receive healing as a special gift of faith for a healing or a miracle.

Healing by your faith in Jesus

Luke 8: As He went, the people crowded Him. 43 And a woman having a hemorrhage for twelve years, who had spent all her living on physicians, but could not be healed by anyone, 44 came behind Him, and touched the fringe of His garment. And immediately her hemorrhage dried up.

45 Jesus said, "Who touched Me?"

When everyone denied it, Peter and those who were with Him said, "Master, the crowds are pressing against You, and You say, 'Who touched Me?' "

46 But Jesus said, "Someone touched Me, for I perceive that power has gone out from Me."

47 When the woman saw that she was not hidden, she came trembling. And falling down before Him, she declared to Him before all the people why she had touched Him and how she was healed immediately. 48 Then He said to her, "Daughter, be of good cheer. Your faith has made you well. Go in peace."

Resurrection of Jairus' daughter

Sometimes, the answer for healing does not come in an expected way. For instance, Jairus was a Jewish leader. He knew about Jesus and went to him to compel him to come pray for his daughter that she might be healed. Jesus agreed to go. Right at this point, while they are passing through the crowd, is when the woman with the issue of blood touches Jesus. It stops Jesus. Rather than Jesus swiftly running to help Jairus's daughter, Jesus stops because of the woman who is healed by faith. I believe it could have caused Jairus to doubt that Jesus understood the urgency of the situation. Right afterwards someone from Jairus' place comes and tells Jairus not to bother Jesus because his daughter has died. Getting news that someone has died is something that certainly could end any faith that he had but Jesus speaks directly to Jairus and encourages him to 'only believe' and his daughter will be made whole. Jesus continues with Jairus and there are people weeping and crying about the child's death. Jesus sends all of the people out of the house and speaks over the body of the girl. He speaks to her spirit commanding her to rise up. She is quickened and she is raised from the dead. This of course causes tremendous joy within the home and family and friends.

There are occurrences where you will need God to speak to you to encourage your faith. For instance, I have been in situations with people near to death. The doctor may say there is no hope, but God's Spirit will quicken a scripture to you to encourage you to believe anyway. These scriptures may come to you directly or can come through the voice of a family member or friend who can use the gift of encouragement to quicken your spirit.

Jesus spoke words of faith to Jairus – to encourage his faith. If someone you know is in a situation near impossible, pray that God will use you to sow words of hope into the person's life.

Also, should you be in a situation that seems impossible, pray asking God to quicken scriptures to you so that your faith can be ignited. Nothing is impossible for God (Matthew 19: 26).

Luke 8: 50 But when Jesus heard it, He answered him, "Do not fear. Only believe, and she will be made well."

51 When He came into the house, He permitted no one to go in except Peter, John and James, and the father and mother of the girl. 52 All wept and mourned for her. But He said, "Do not weep. She is not dead but sleeping."

53 They laughed at Him, knowing that she was dead. 54 But He put them all outside and took her by the hand and called, saying, "Little girl, arise." 55 Her spirit returned, and she arose immediately. And He told them to give her food. 56 Her parents were astonished, but He commanded them to tell no one what had happened

God will use you

There are instances that may come to you where you can pray healing for a person. Jesus gave authority to all his disciples to preach, cast out demons, heal the sick, pray in tongues and be able to handle deadly situations with faith. What it means is even if you don't flow in the gifts of healing, use your believer's authority to pray and lay hands on the sick that they might be healed. I truly believe that if you are in such a situation where life or death is an issue, you are not there by coincidence. God has you there so you can be as Jesus reaching into someone's life bringing healing and life.

I was dining at a fast food restaurant, a normal day on my lunch break. I noticed people, but was not really paying much attention until I saw a man a woman and child carrying their trays to be seated near me What happened is that suddenly the man hit the ground. I observed. He didn't try to get up. I knew I should do something. It was seconds only; I got up and approached the woman and asked if I could pray for the man. She said yes. I kneeled next to him and prayed in the name of Jesus that he would be well and within several minutes the man rose up, sat at the table and had his lunch with his family. I don't know what it was about. I didn't even stay to get health facts or whatever. I knew without a doubt, my being there was not a coincidence. I was willing to be used by God. I know God can heal because of the Word of God. I also know because I have been healed more than once myself. I truly believe it was believer's authority as Jesus promises in the scripture.

These signs shall follow believers

Mark 16: 15 He said to them, "Go into all the world, and preach the gospel to every creature. 16 He who believes and is baptized will be saved. But he who does not believe will be condemned. 17 These signs will accompany those who believe: In My name they will cast out demons; they will speak with new tongues; 18 they will take up serpents; if they drink any deadly thing, it will not hurt them; they will lay hands on the sick, and they will recover."

There are instances when a person needs healing but the root of the illness is spiritual – a demonic disease. The only way you will know it is by the Holy Spirit of God. You will discern with your spirit that an evil spirit is attacking the person or keeping him or her in bondage. For instance, the boy in the scripture below. It was diagnosed as epilepsy but it was a demonic spirit binding him. In such an instance, you must rebuke the demon: bind him and cast him out. As Jesus did it, the boy was immediately healed.

Cast out demons and brought healing – Jesus faith appealed to mercy

Matthew 17: 14 When they came to the crowd, a man came to Him and knelt before Him, saying, 15 "Lord, have mercy on my son, for he is an epileptic and suffers terribly. He often falls into the fire and often into the water. 16 I brought him to Your disciples, but they could not heal him."

17 Then Jesus answered, "O faithless and perverse generation, how long shall I be with you? How long shall I bear with you? Bring him here to Me." 18 Jesus rebuked the demon, and he came out of him. And the child was healed instantly.

19 Then the disciples came to Jesus privately and said, "Why could we not cast him out?"

20 Jesus said to them, "Because of your unbelief. For truly I say to you, if you have faith as a grain of mustard seed, you will say to this mountain, 'Move from here to there,' and it will move. And nothing will be impossible for you. 21 But this kind does not go out except by prayer and fasting."

There are people who need to know that it is God's will to heal them because they do not know the scriptures or the truth about Jesus the healer. They may think they are not good enough to be healed. If they don't know the scriptures, they certainly won't know how good God is. Leprosy is a horrible disease; the people who had it could not go in public places or they would risk death. Yet a leper went to Jesus. He obviously had some faith. His faith though was conditional.

He didn't know how good Jesus really was. He said, "If it be your will". He knew Jesus could heal but maybe didn't think Jesus would heal anyone. The man should not even have been a public place. Jesus not only says it is his will to heal, he reaches out and touches the man with leprosy and heals the man completely. Rather than catch the leprosy, which is what all people would believe, Jesus imparted healing. The man's life was radically transformed. He could return home to his loved ones. He could work and be in public without fear.

He expressed His will to heal.

Luke 5: 12 When He was in a certain city, a man full of leprosy, upon seeing Jesus, fell on his face and begged Him, "Lord, if You will, You can make me clean."

13 He reached out His hand and touched him, saying, "I will. Be clean." And immediately the leprosy left him.

14 Then He commanded him to tell no one, "But go and show yourself to the priest and make an offering for your cleansing, as Moses commanded, as a testimony to them."

15 Yet even more so His fame went everywhere. And great crowds came together to hear and to be healed by Him of their infirmities. 16 But He withdrew to the wilderness and prayed.

Healing of the lame man

Peter and John

Peter and John were on their way to the temple to pray. They saw a lame man who was begging. Peter says to him "look at us". The man looks expecting to receive. He was probably hoping it was money. Peter tells him what he has to give – healing. Peter commands him in the name of Jesus to rise up and walk. The man stands up and starts jumping for joy because he is completely healed. Sometimes, what the person expects is not what you are there to give. I am not against giving to people in need. Sometimes though, God would completely heal the people and they will no longer need to be poor.

Acts 3: 3 Now Peter and John went up together to the temple at the ninth hour, the hour of prayer. 2 A man lame from birth was being carried, whom people placed daily at the gate of the temple called Beautiful to ask alms from those who entered the temple. 3 Seeing Peter and John about to go into the temple, he asked for alms. 4 Peter, gazing at him with John, said, "Look at us." 5 So he paid attention to them, expecting to receive something from them.

6 Then Peter said, "I have no silver and gold, but I give you what I have. In the name of Jesus Christ of Nazareth, rise up and walk." 7 He took him by the right hand and raised him up. Immediately his feet and ankles were strengthened. 8 Jumping up, he stood and walked and entered the temple with them, walking and jumping and praising God. 9 All the people saw him walking and praising God. 10 They knew that it was he who sat for alms at the Beautiful Gate of the temple. And they were filled with wonder and amazement at what happened to him.

Examples of Healing

Faith comes by hearing and hearing by the word of God. The word of God spoken over a person with faith ignites faith in the person and brings healing or miracles or answers to prayer. It is necessary that a person get the Word of God on the inward parts of his or her being. It is important to read the Word of God daily and prayerfully so that God can quicken you to receive it.

As you read the word, say it, pray it and receive it as God's will for your life, it becomes a living part of you. The engrafted word is able to save the soul (James 1: 21). The word of God that you literally receive into your soul, into your spirit becomes RHEMA or inspired. That means it becomes a living word on the inside of you. Faith and the word of God produce miracles (Hebrews 4: 2). If the need should arise for a miracle, the word of God will rise up from your spirit and speak it with faith and boldness. The Word must be mixed with faith to produce life. Faith comes by hearing the word.

Faith to be healed – faith comes from hearing and hearing by the word

There are several ministries that have CD's of healing scriptures. You can let them play next to someone's bed while he or she is recovering. Hearing the word of God while you need strength is the best possible solution. I have recorded some scriptures for my own self that if I should need to hear words of encouragement and faith imparted, I can listen to my own voice reading those scriptures with faith.

Hebrews 11: 6 And without faith it is impossible to please God, for he who comes to God must believe that He exists and that He is a rewarder of those who diligently seek Him.

Romans 10: 17 So then faith comes by hearing, and hearing by the word of God.

Get the Word of God into your spirit
Listen to it, read it, play it, confess it – align with God's Word

How important the word of God should be to you

The Word of God should be our first resource for all life. Knowing the Word of God only comes through reading it, praying it and believing it. Confess it. God instructed Moses to teach the Israelites that the Word of

God must be first in their lives. Some Jews literally wear phylacteries, or little compartments they tie on their heads and arms that contain the scriptures. They do it as an outward sign of what they believe. They believe that Word of God is so important they place it on their bodies. There is life and strength, health and healing in God's Word. Keep the Word of God as a priority in your life.

Deuteronomy 11: 18 Therefore you must fix these words of mine in your heart and in your soul, and bind them as a sign on your hand, so that they may be as frontlets between your eyes. 19 You shall teach them to your children, speaking of them when you sit in your house and when you walk by the way, when you lie down, and when you rise up. 20 You shall write them on the doorposts of your house and on your gates, 21 so that your days and the days of your children may be multiplied in the land which the Lord swore to your fathers to give them, as long as the days of heaven on the earth.

22 For if you diligently keep all these commandments which I am commanding you to do—to love the Lord your God, to walk in all His ways, and to hold fast to Him— 23 then the Lord will drive out all these nations from before you, and you will dispossess nations greater and mightier than you. 24 Every place where the soles of your feet tread will be yours. Your border will be from the wilderness to Lebanon, from the river, the River Euphrates, as far as the Mediterranean Sea. 25 No man will be able to resist you, for the Lord your God shall lay the fear of you and the dread of you on all the land where you shall tread, just as He has spoken to you.

26 See, I am setting before you today a blessing and a curse: 27 the blessing if you obey the commandments of the Lord your God, which I am commanding you today, 28 and the curse, if you will not obey the commandments of the Lord your God, but turn from the way which I am commanding you today, to go after other gods which you have not known.
Faith – believe receive – come into agreement with God's word

On the healing of the boy with the demon, the disciples had tried to heal him but could not. Jesus had given them authority to heal. Jesus corrects the, and says if they had even a tiny seed of faith, they would speak in authority and a mountain would move, that nothing would be impossible for them. He also adds that for some instances such as this a lifestyle of combined prayer and fasting is necessary to impart healing. Prayer and fasting should be the lifestyle of a Christian.

Matthew 17: 20 Jesus said to them, "Because of your unbelief. For truly I say to you, if you have faith as a grain of mustard seed, you will say to this mountain, 'Move from here to there,' and it will move. And nothing will be impossible for you. 21 But this kind does not go out except by prayer and fasting."

Prayer of faith

Only you decide what you should do. I've been a part of churches that occasionally fasted. I've been a part of churches who fasted monthly. I know of churches that fast weekly. They do it to honour God. It can be a fasting from all food and drink. It can be a fasting from desserts or meat. It can be a fasting from solid foods. There are some excellent books on fasting. Jentzen Franklyn has some excellent books on this topic. International House of Prayer also has excellent teachings on the topic. It is not that your fasting makes you holier or worthier. What it does is get you to pray more and to focus on God with all your being. If you have never fasted, consider reading some Biblical resources that can help you to understand it.

HEALINGS
Instant

Most of the examples I have given in this chapter have been of instant or immediate healings. Sometimes though healing can occur in increments. There is an occasion where a second touch from Jesus is required to complete the healing. Some healings are progressive.

Increments as they went they were healed

Jesus was passing by and a group of lepers saw him at a distance and cried out for mercy from him. The lepers together cried out. Jesus spoke words that encouraged them completely. When Jesus said "go show yourself" to the priests, he was saying you are healed. Lepers could not return to their families until they had proven they were healed by going to the priests who were trained to look for signs of the disease. All of them started on their way to the priests. The scriptures say "as they went" they were healed. (Leviticus 14)

Luke 17: 11 As Jesus went to Jerusalem, He passed between Samaria and Galilee. 12 As He entered a village, there met Him ten men who were lepers, who stood at a distance. 13 They lifted up their voices, saying, "Jesus, Master, have pity on us!"

14 When He saw them, He said to them, "Go, show yourselves to the priests." And as they went, they were cleansed.

I have received this type of healing myself. I went prayerfully to church although I was not well. I went for prayer believing that I would be healed. I had been healed before so I knew God is merciful. I also know the scriptures about healing. As the minister was praying for me, anointing me with oil, I felt like a push through my spirit. It's hard to explain. I knew that in my spirit something had happened. As I got to my seat, I felt no better. I announced to my friends I would not be able to stay and must go home. I do believe that both my friends prayed for me even though they didn't say anything. As I was driving towards home, suddenly I realized I felt well. I realized I had been completely healed. I announced it and my friends rejoiced with me.

Healing by a second touch

There is a special instance given where one touch from Jesus only brought partial healing. The reasons aren't given but are assumed. The place of Bethsaida must not have been a place of faith at all, because Jesus takes the man who wants healing outside of the town. Jesus spit on him. This is similar to the other instance of the blind man.

Jesus questions him and wants to know if the man can see. The man describes a blurred type of vision. Jesus touches him once more and lays hands on him. The blind man is completely healed. Jesus warns him not to go back to the town or to tell anyone in the town. It is possible that unbelief in a place or a people can limit the working of miracles and healings. There may be instances in your life, where you will be lead to a different place or a different source than your usual church for healing. It is possible that you may receive partial healing and then complete healing.

Mark 8: 22 He came to Bethsaida. And they brought a blind man to Him and entreated Him to touch him. 23 He took the blind man by the hand and led him out of the town. When He had spit on his eyes and put His hands on him, He asked him, "Do you see anything?"

24 He looked up and said, "I see men as trees, walking."

25 Then again He put His hands on his eyes and made him look up. And he was restored and saw everyone clearly. 26 He sent him home away to his house, saying, "Neither go into the town, nor tell it to anyone in the town."

Healing of many by laying on of hands

In some instances, the laying on of hands is necessary. Believers lay hands on believing people. In the occasion below he healed all of them that he layed hands on. I have been in many services and healing crusades where there was prayer for healing. I saw many people healed. I was in a meeting where two of my friends received healing and 3 of them were slain in the Spirit. I saw hundreds of people go to the front to give their testimony of receiving healing. I cannot say that I have yet seen every person who was in a meeting receive his or her healing but I believe for it. If Jesus did it and gave us the authority to heal the sick, I am believing for the a revival of faith in the Church so that in the meeting, all people with a need will be healed, saved or delivered or receive the miracle they desire.

Luke 4: 40 Now when the sun was setting, all those who had anyone sick with various diseases brought them to Him. And He laid His hands on every one of them and healed them. 41 And demons came out of many, crying out, "You are the Christ, the Son of God!" But He rebuked them and did not permit them to speak, because they knew that He was the Christ.

Jesus commissioned the 12 to do the same

This passage shows that Jesus had the authority to give the disciples authority to heal. This is while he is on earth. He commissioned them, before his death to do the works of God.

Matthew 10: 10 He called His twelve disciples to Him and gave them authority over unclean spirits, to cast them out, and to heal all kinds of sickness and all kinds of disease.

Matthew 10: 2 Now the names of the twelve apostles are these: first, Simon, who is called Peter, and Andrew, his brother; James, the son of Zebedee, and John, his brother; 3 Philip and Bartholomew; Thomas, and Matthew, the tax collector; James, the son of Alphaeus; and Lebbaeus, whose surname was Thaddaeus; 4 Simon the Zealot; and Judas Iscariot, who also betrayed Him.

The Commissioning of the Twelve Apostles

Matthew 10: 5 These twelve Jesus sent out, and commanded them, saying, "Do not go into the way of the Gentiles, and do not enter any city of the

Samaritans. 6 But go rather to the lost sheep of the house of Israel. 7 As you go, preach, saying, 'The kingdom of heaven is at hand.' 8 Heal the sick, cleanse the lepers, raise the dead, and cast out demons. Freely you have received, freely give.

The Great commission

After the resurrection of Jesus, and before his ascension into heaven. Jesus commands the disciple to preach the gospel and to teach it until He returns. Not only does it to get them to do the works of God but He says it is necessary to reach all people groups on earth until he returns or at the end of the age. This command is not only to the twelve but to all believers. As long as we live on earth, we should be sharing Christ with people. It is the main reason we are on earth. Yes, God wants us to enjoy the pleasures of life, but it is not instead of sharing Jesus. All people have circles of influence through their career, hobbies, leisure activities, churches etc. We may be the only Christians some of these people will ever know. The commission if for us to do whatever we can to share Jesus with people.

Matthew 28: 18 Then Jesus came and spoke to them, saying, "All authority has been given to Me in heaven and on earth. 19 Go therefore and make disciples of all nations, baptizing them in the name of the Father and of the Son and of the Holy Spirit, 20 teaching them to observe all things I have commanded you. And remember, I am with you always, even to the end of the age." Amen.

Miracles, signs, wonders, healings

The apostles and disciples did as Jesus commanded. Crowds of people gathered around them so that they could be healed. People came to the disciples knowing the anointing that was on Jesus, the Holy Spirit, was upon them. It literally says that even the shadow of the Apostle Peter would bring healing to those desiring a healing or miracle. Some are called to Evangelize for their career in ministry. They have special gifts to help them. They will often have the gifts of healing and working of miracles. If possible, get into meetings with those anointed for ministry even if you don't need it for yourself. You can see the gifts of healing manifest and can be a witness to salvation, healing and deliverance. It could build up your faith so that you may pray for people to bring healing.

Acts 5: 12 Many signs and wonders were performed among the people by the hands of the apostles. And they were all together in Solomon's Porch. 13 No one else dared join them, but the people respected them. 14

Believers were increasingly added to the Lord, crowds of both men and women, 15 so that they even brought the sick out into the streets and placed them on beds and mats, that at least the shadow of Peter passing by might touch some of them. 16 Crowds also came out of the cities surrounding Jerusalem, bringing the sick and those who were afflicted by evil spirits, and they were all healed.

Paul heals Eutychus

The Apostle Paul was well educated in both Hebrew and Greek and Latin. He was radically transformed by his encounter with Jesus Christ. He stopped persecuting Christians, became a radical Christian and went about healing and preaching and teaching Jesus the Saviour. He was known for his teaching gift and his "long speaking". He would preach long because he knew what he had to share was important and that he may not get to come back to the place. On one of his long preaching sprees, Eutychus who was listening dozed off and feel out of a window ledge. He died. Paul rushed out and Eutychus became healed and was able to rejoice with his friends

.

This healing miracle is important because Paul was not one of the 12 disciples. He never knew Jesus on earth. He was used to bring healing, the resurrection of the dead and the message of the gospel to people. The same anointing on the disciples is ours once we are baptized in the Holy Spirit. God will use us to share Jesus Christ with people. It may not be your career but God will use you in the realms of your influence to make a difference.

Acts 20: 10 Paul went down and leaned over him, and embracing him said, "Do not be troubled, for he is alive." 11 When he had gone up and had broken bread and eaten, he conversed for a long while until dawn and departed. 12 They took the lad in alive and were greatly comforted.

In this next healing, the Apostle Peter is used to bring healing to someone who was paralyzed. Some people believe that if you haven't been healed by a certain period, perhaps you will never be healed. It is not the case. The faith encounter Peter has with Aenas commands him to rise up and he does and those who lived in the area all became Christians because of it. God can use signs and wonders to draw people to himself. There are people who are desperate for a cure for themselves or others. They will go to a healing meeting, even if they are not believers. God will sometimes heal a person so that all the person'e family and friends will become Christians.

Acts 9: 32 The Healing of Aeneas

32 As Peter passed through every region, he came down also to the saints who lived in Lydda. 33 There he found a man named Aeneas, who had been bedridden for eight years and was paralyzed. 34 Peter said to him, "Aeneas, Jesus the Christ heals you. Rise up and make your bed." And immediately he rose up. 35 All those who lived in Lydda and Sharon saw him and turned to the Lord.

In the following example, Peter resurrects the woman Dorcas. The people were weeping for her, but Peter commanded her to rise from the dead. She did. I believe in the resurrection of the dead. I also believe that if a person dies in my presence, I should pray or command the person (obeying the Holy Spirit's leading) to rise from the dead. It is not my own faith or my own power. Please see that you or I as a believer in Christ can be used by the Holy Spirit. It is a matter of letting the Holy Spirit use you.

Healing of Dorcas

Acts 9: 6 In Joppa there was a disciple named Tabitha, which is translated Dorcas. This woman was full of good works and almsgiving. 37 In those days she became ill and died. And when they had washed her, they placed her in an upper room. 38 Since Lydda was near Joppa, the disciples, hearing that Peter was there, sent two men to him, pleading, "Do not delay to come to us."

39 Peter rose up and went with them. When he arrived, they led him into the upper room. All the widows stood by him weeping, and showing the tunics and garments which Dorcas had made while she was with them.

40 Peter put them all outside and knelt down and prayed. And turning to the body he said, "Tabitha, arise." She opened her eyes, and when she saw Peter she sat up. 41 He gave her his hand and lifted her up. And when he had called the saints and widows, he presented her alive. 42 It became known throughout all Joppa, and many believed in the Lord. 43 He remained in Joppa for many days with Simon, a tanner.

The Apostle Paul was sentenced for preaching the gospel and put in jail. The Jewish leaders of the day hated him because he had been one of them and now was teaching and preaching Christ.

After enduring a horrible storm and shipwreck, Paul and the other prisoners and the Romans swam to an island nearby. The Apostle Paul healed people as he was on that island.

Acts 28: 7 In that area was an estate of the chief man of the island, named
Publius, who had welcomed us and courteously housed us for three days. 8
It happened that the father of Publius lay sick with a fever and dysentery.
Paul visited him and, placing his hands on him, prayed and healed him. 9
When this happened, the rest on the island who had diseases also came and
were healed. 10 They honored us in many ways. And when we sailed, they
provided us with necessary supplies.

Should you receive healing

Thank God for it immediately. Thanking God for it is the right thing to do. God has brought about the miracle. If a preacher or elder was used to pray for you, it is Jesus that healed you. Immediately confess with your mouth 'Thank you God for healing me.' Receive it in your spirit and say over yourself " I receive complete and total healing in Jesus name.' That is taking hold of it in the spirit.

There are some people who do not thank God. I know it is hard to believe but it is true. The example is shown in the instance with the lepers who were healed. Jesus spoke a word and they were healed as they went. Only one of them returned to thank Jesus. Their lives had been completely transformed. They no longer had to live in isolation. They were free to be with family and friends. They could pursue a job. Their lives were completely changed. Only one went to Jesus to thank him.

1 leper returned

After Jesus has sent a word of faith to heal the lepers, and they were healed as they went, one leper returned to thank Jesus. Jesus speaks words to encourage him and says your faith has made you well. I believe that leper had special revelation that Jesus was more than just a man. He returned to thank him because he realized the authority in Jesus.

Luke 17: 17 Jesus said, "Were not the ten cleansed? Where are the nine? 18
Were there not any found to return and give glory to God except this
foreigner?" 19 Then He said to him, "Rise, go your way. Your faith has
made you well."

Give your testimony

After you thank God, give your testimony. If you are in a meeting and the minister gives room for people to tell if God has healed them, you should go and speak what God has done for you. Sometimes in those types of situations, as you give your testimony, it causes others to believe God for healing for themselves. If God has healed you, tell others to inspire them. God will bring people in your life that you can share your testimony with who can be healed or have faith to pray for loved ones who need healing.

Sow a seed into healing ministries

You do not have to do this thing, but if you have been healed, you will want to do it. Sow a seed into healing ministries. There are ministries that preach and teach healing. By sowing, I mean give financially but also prayerfully over those ministries. It can be a onetime gift or you may feel a desire from God to give frequently to them. As you give, you partner with those ministers who teach and preach Christ. You receive part of the blessing of winning souls and doing the works of God by your giving in faith. The same anointing that is on those ministries can come in your life. Give with a sincere desire to see others saved, healed and delivered and you will reap a spiritual blessing from God.

Galatians 6: 7 Be not deceived. God is not mocked. For whatever a man sows, that will he also reap. 8 For the one who sows to his own flesh will from the flesh reap corruption, but the one who sows to the Spirit will from the Spirit reap eternal life.

Freewill offering

Don't give because someone says you must give. If someone says you must give to be healed, the person is not pure in heart. Jesus said freely you receive so freely give. You do not give financially to get a healing; you give to thank God in faith for what God has given you. Also, if you were healed because of a minister on television or the Internet, write that person a special letter of testimony to encourage him or her. God can use a minister on television to pray and you receive blessing.

There are faithful spirit filled evangelists that pray for people in their broadcasts, and not everyone writes them to thank them for their ministry. Do it. Thank God for them preaching and teaching the good news. Your testimony will encourage them.

Leviticus 22: 17 The Lord spoke to Moses, saying: 18 Speak to Aaron, and to his sons, and to all the children of Israel, and say to them: Whoever from the house of Israel or from the foreigners in Israel who offers his burnt

offering for any vows or freewill offerings that he offers to the Lord, 19
then if it is to be accepted for you, the offering shall be a male without blemish, a bull, sheep, or goat.

Thanksgiving offering

Leviticus 22: 29 When you offer a sacrifice of thanksgiving to the Lord, offer it so that it may be accepted. 30 On the same day it shall be eaten. You shall leave none of it until the next day: I am the Lord.

5 RECEIVING YOUR HEALING

Receiving your healing
Chapter 5

The Prayer of Faith

Faith is the necessary element that brings healing. It could be your faith because you have heard the preached word or God has quickened a scripture to you. It could be the faith of the minister praying for you. It could be the faith of people who are praying for you. Faith is only way that healing is released.

Romans 10: 17 Consequently, faith comes from hearing the message, and the message is heard through the word about Christ.

Prayer of Faith – from my book on Kinds of prayer

The Word of God has within itself the power to bring itself to come to pass by releasing faith into believers as it is spoken or preached. The hearing that is talked about is not hearing with only your natural ears but hearing with your spiritual ears. It means your heart has been softened to receive the Word of God as truth and you grab onto it mixed with faith and accept it as a personal truth from God to you. A transference occurs from you saying ‘ yes I know it is true’ to believing that it is true and applies directly to you.

I can explain it by explaining an example of someone who resists it. I was praying for the baptism of the Holy Spirit for someone; we were praying for a class that had been water baptized and taught the truths about the baptism of the Holy Spirit. As with anything spiritual, God will never force you to believe it; you must always have an active part of believing and receiving. I was praying for this woman and the woman had her teeth clenched, her arms folded, her body posture completely closed as though she were trying to protect herself.

She kept on saying " I don't want it. I don't want it. I don't want it." It would have been ridiculous for me to pray for her because she did not want the Baptism of the Holy Spirit. If someone pits his or her human will against something – leave that person alone. God will never force Himself. Even though the Word of God was taught and preached about the truths of the Baptism of the Holy Spirit, even though people all around her were receiving the baptism of the Holy Spirit with speaking in other tongues, she did not receive the word of God with faith. She rejected it and pit herself against it.

In the same manner, as the sermon is preached or the Word of God is read aloud and you hear it with your physical ears, you have a chance to reject it by making excuses, to believe it is nice like elevator music or to receive it with faith. God's Word always brings personal decision making as it is taught or preached.

Align yourself with God's Word

If you go for prayer for divine healing, you cannot speak words like 'Nothing happened. I know nothing happened.' Or other words that express unbelief. You must align yourself with God's Word and say things like " The prayer of faith will heal the sick." Align yourself in the core of your being to the Word of God.

Believing it is true for you is a big part of getting something from the teaching or preaching. You speaking a word of faith out of your own mouth, speaking it quickened by faith is the best way for you to receive anything from God. You are your own best teacher. That is why we confess the promises of God to us; that is why we pray the Word of God for us. In Joshua 1, God instructs Israel to keep the Word of God before them day and night. God impresses upon Moses, later on Joshua the importance of memorizing the scriptures and keeping them in mind. In the Old Testament, and today by Orthodox Jews, they literally attach the scripture in boxes around their foreheads and around their hands. These boxes, phylacteries, contain the scriptures – always the commandments but sometimes more. This is a symbol of what they are doing inwardly – keeping God's word as top priority.

Although I don't wear them on my arms or forehead, I do sometimes carry scriptures with me in my pocket or place it on my mirror or in the car so I will read it, pray it and study it. I have been known to receive a message from church and buy the tape or the CD and play it over and over again for weeks until the truths are deep in my heart. I also have boxes of index cards with promises of God that I am believing God for. I use them to pray, one card after the other. I don't always read all of them but they are there to remind me of what God has promised me as a prompt in prayer and

speaking to you from His Word. God uses preachers and teachers but also, you could be reading the scriptures and it will jump at you and you know God is speaking to you.

The Word of God is the guide book for life on earth. It applies to every aspect of our human life. It was written so that God could share His heart with us about what pleases Him and what to avoid etc. It's a book for how to live a godly life on the planet Earth. The Word produces in us fruitfulness. The book of Deuteronomy speaks of the blessings of the LORD for those who honour Him and serve Him. Read this book prayerfully. Receive it as for you personally. It explains the blessings God wants to give to His people. Deuteronomy 28 gives a list of the blessings of following God and curses should you not honour the Lord.

God Wants you to Live in the Blessing

I mention this book of Deuteronomy because some people actually take vows of poverty believing that it makes them more holy. God's desire has always been to prosper us so much that we are able to be a blessing to those around us. He calls us trees of righteousness, the planting of the LORD (Is 61) so that we might share with those who have nothing and so that we can give to ministry and evangelism. God wants us to live in the blessing – that means the protection and provision for His people.

Deuteronomy 28: 2 All these blessings will come on you and accompany
you if you obey the LORD your God: 3 You will be blessed in the city and
blessed in the country.
4 The fruit of your womb will be blessed, and the crops of your land and the young of your livestock—the calves of your herds and the lambs of your flocks.
5 Your basket and your kneading trough will be blessed.
6 You will be blessed when you come in and blessed when you go out.
7 The LORD will grant that the enemies who rise up against you will be defeated before you. They will come at you from one direction but flee from you in seven.

These scriptures show that God wants to bless you in all these areas of your life. Do you believe it? Do you receive it? You've got to believe it is God's will for you and you've got to receive it.

These are the blessings of the Old Testament. These are the blessings given to Moses. How much more has the blood of Christ made us joint heirs with Jesus? We can pray with confidence knowing His blood made the way for us to enter the Holiest place. These scriptures are for us to take personally. They apply to us. We have been engrafted into the side of Jesus Christ – now made an heir with Jesus of all the promises of God to Abraham, Isaac, Jacob, Moses etc.

Literally praying these scriptures over yourself in faith believing that God will give you these things He has promised is essential. You must believe that He has given them to us and that He wants us to have them. It is not only financial though. The blessings of God are for every area of your life. It includes spiritual revitalization and physical health. Praying the kind of prayers that the apostle Paul prayed will get you results in other areas of your life also.

Ephesians 1: 15 For this reason, ever since I heard about your faith in the Lord Jesus and your love for all God's people, 16 I have not stopped giving thanks for you, remembering you in my prayers. 17 I keep asking that the God of our Lord Jesus Christ, the glorious Father, may give you the Spirit[f] of wisdom and revelation, so that you may know him better. 18 I pray that the eyes of your heart may be enlightened in order that you may know the hope to which he has called you, the riches of his glorious inheritance in his holy people, 19 and his incomparably great power for us who believe.

Seek God Wholly

Yes. Pray and confess the scriptures on healing, but also pray over the other areas of your life. Seek God with all your being for your spirit, soul and body. This is a type of thanksgiving prayer thanking God for the people and also an intercessory prayer praying for spiritual revelation. This is praying for God to reveal His glory to you. This is a prayer to pray over yourself. Pray that God would help you to understand more of the Word of God. Pray that you might know Him more. Ask God for wisdom, knowledge and revelation. Expect for Him to impart it to you.

The Holy Spirit will release new measures of the glory of God to you. Ask and believe that God will give you wisdom. There are depths in the riches of the glory of Christ. If you earnestly desire more of God, He will continuously transform you from glory to glory.

I pray for wisdom for all parts of my life. I want words of wisdom for me at school. I want words of wisdom in the community. I want words of wisdom in the church. I want them at home. Don't only believe it is for one thing alone. God's Word can apply to all areas of your life. There can be a

100-fold increase of God's Word applied to all areas of your life as you apply God's scriptures with revelation. This comes through praying the scriptures and taking them personally.

God gives us blessings for all areas of our lives physical, financial, for your soul, for your relationships etc. As we begin to pray to apply God's word to our lives, God will increase our capacity to receive from Him in those areas.

Increase your capacity to receive

I want to express it to you such as this; a cup can hold a cup of water. My tap turned on flows more than a cupful. I could use a pot and it would hold more water. I could use a bathtub; it would be more. The truth is I could fill a swimming pool with water from a tap. With God, there is no limit to what He can or will do for us. It depends on our capacity to receive. We should literally pray for God to increase our capacity to receive. This will mean God will grow us in such a way that we can learn more about him and be able to receive more from Him.

As you are praying for your healing to manifest, also ask God to fill you to overflowing in your spirit. Also ask God for insight and revelation about God's Word. As you are praying, Jesus is the author of your faith (Hebrews 12: 2). Jesus is the high priest (Hebrews 4: 14-16) over your profession of faith. Jesus is not only passively hearing your prayers. He is giving you faith as you read the word, pray the word and confess the word. Jesus is also your prayer partner. His blood gave Him the authority to be your LORD. It made a way for you to enter into the Throne room of God. Jesus is interceding for you. Your responsibility to read the word, confess the Word and pray the Word.

There was a time in my life where I made faith tapes for myself. I taped scriptures I was believing God for and played them over and over so the Word would get on the inside of me. Even people in a coma can receive the word of God. The spirit is quickened by the Word of God. I have prayed over people in a coma, and spoken prayers of faith over them, knowing they could not hear me with their physical ears but their spirits could receive. There are so many ministries that have scriptures on CDS or tapes for you to play to get the Word of God on the inside of you but let me share with you; your own voice speaking the Word of God with faith is the strongest influence on your own life. Listen to the voice you can believe in.

Some people find it hard to memorize scripture, so a technique to help you would be to turn it into song. Sing it. If you don't know how to create a melody, take a melody you already know and sing the scripture to it.

Get in the Word of God

In order for something extraordinary to occur such as a healing or miracle, you've got to get the Word of God in you more than ever before. Read the Word; listen to the Word. Make the Word of God the primary source you use each day. Many people casually turn on the television as soon as they enter a room; you decide to turn to the scriptures as soon as you go into a room.

As a new Christian, I would read the Bible in spurts on my own. Soon, a teacher introduced me to the read through the Bible in a year Bible and it made me more of a consistent reader of the Word. As I grew in Christ, I began to want to read through the Bible more than once a year. I wanted to study it in chunks. I became quite passionate about the Word the more I studied it, and even in my secular job, I would bring a Bible and at lunch, I would lock my door and read the Bible. I wanted the Word more than I wanted the gossip at work. I wanted the Word more than I wanted anything else. I would dig into parts of scripture and I found God was quickening the scriptures to me more throughout my day. I would be talking with someone at my job and I would speak the scripture to people in words of wisdom, or words of encouragement.

What this does, getting the scripture on the inside of you as I call it is build your faith to receive from God so that when you pray, you can pray with wisdom (knowing what God's Word states) and faith believing the Word and knowing the God who can bring it to pass.

I encourage you to make a spiritual investment in your own spiritual life. You must get the Word of God into you yourself. Buy yourself CDs, DVDs, music etc. that will help to build up your spirit. Get the ones on healing but also get others on faith and believing God for miracles. Faith based teaching is what you must get in you to quicken your faith, Read the Bible prayerfully.

Build up your faith by praying scripture over your situations or people. As you pray the Word of God over yourself and others, you release faith in the scripture; more faith is released as you hear yourself praying the prayer of faith. It not only is praying God's will for somebody, but it is building you up in the faith.

The Prayer of Faith – can be prayed with confidence knowing it is God's will because it is in the Word. The prayer of faith arise from your spirit where you know you have received from God and you may only need pray that prayer once. Usually elders or ministers pray the prayer of faith over you and anoint you with oil. You can pray it yourself for yourself, but the prayer must arise from your spirit. If you don't know the difference between a prayer from your soul and a prayer from your spirit, you could pray in tongues over yourself. You should also get ministers to pray for you and anoint you with oil.

Often only needed one prayer

There are situations where you may pray the prayer of faith over a situation and it will immediately be answered. I mean it may manifest in the natural realm almost immediately. There are other times that you pray the prayer of faith and you know that you have received the answer by faith. Start praising God and thanking Him for the answer. If you know that you have the answer (by the spirit) start thanking God and keep thanking Him and praising Him until you see the answer manifest in the natural.

Usually gift of faith is used with this prayer

In special situations such as a life or death situation, or destiny decision, God grants us the gift of faith. This is more than ordinary faith that is released by hearing the Word of God. The gift of faith is supernatural faith through the Holy Spirit to believe for miracles.

James 5: 13-15

13 Is anyone among you in trouble? Let them pray. Is anyone happy? Let
them sing songs of praise. 14 Is anyone among you sick? Let them call the
elders of the church to pray over them and anoint them with oil in the
name of the Lord. 15 And the prayer offered in faith will make the sick
person well; the Lord will raise them up. If they have sinned, they will be
forgiven.

The scripture instructs us on how to minister to the sick. The elders or mature Christians should pray over them anointing them with oil which is a symbol of the Holy Spirit. They are to pray for healing. They are not to wonder if the person will live or die. The prayer of faith prays God's Word. Jesus healed the sick. Jesus heals the sick today through those who believe and pray the prayer of faith. I have received this ministry on several occasions in my life. I have also ministered to others this sacrament. You place the oil on the person imparting the life of Christ.

The Holy Spirit using you to be a point of contact laying hands on someone is miraculous. God can impart to you faith for a miracle and through you the healing power of Christ.

Warning: If someone tries to lay hands on you in unbelief – run from them. Do not just let anyone lay hands on you. They should be people known to you as elders in the church or ministers of the LORD. If the person prays in unbelief at all as to whether God wants to heal you or not, get away from that person so he or she cannot touch you. Don't receive a prayer of unbelief over you when you are believing for a miracle. If they are not sure the LORD wants to heal you. Those people got nothing to do with you.

The scripture states the prayer of faith shall save the sick. The prayer of faith – we believe – we literally impart faith for a miracle and the healing power of God. One funny instance I recall is a testimony of a man and his wife who were praying over their baby. They didn't know what to do exactly but they read it in the Bible and believed it so they put their baby in a bathtub and poured a bottle of oil over the kid. The kid was slippery because they put so much oil. God answered their prayer and healed the baby because He saw their faith.

I saw my own mother near death, in a coma, hooked up to machines for breathing, etc. Doctors let me know there was a chance she may not live. I sat there praying and praying. I was praying for a miracle. I believed God would do a miracle. I begged the nurses to let me stay there and pray late into the evenings. I went on my lunch hour. I prayed over her scripture, believing God was there with me – with her. I called everyone I knew that could pray to pray. I sent out prayer requests to ministries. The elders came and prayed for my mum and anointed her with oil. I got a prayer cloth and had it anointed with oil with faith and I pinned it to her hospital gown. Within three days, she was sitting up in her hospital bed taking communion with me. She was off all those life keeping machines except for the heart monitor.

Thank God, I have seen the prayer of faith in action. I told of my Pastor who was on his death bed; the doctors said he probably wouldn't live. They were so negative, any time we heard from them we immediately were bleeding the blood over him and his relatives. We started praying scriptures. In a life or death situation, you cannot be moved by what you hear or what you see. You must believe the Word of God and pray in faith until the natural aligns with God's Word.

Remember those doctors are confined to the 3 dimensions of this earth. We are not confined – we can have confidence to enter the most Holy place the Holy of Holies in Heaven praying to Jesus who paid the price for all sin, sickness, disease etc. by dying on the cross.

The scripture says " If they have sinned, they will be forgiven." The prayer of faith ministers to the spirit, the soul and the body of the person. Jesus ministers to the whole person. We have by faith the anointing to minister healing to all parts of a person. This does not replace repentance by the person, but if the person cannot pray for himself or herself, we can minster in faith.

Forgive

If someone has sinned against you, you have the authority to forgive that person for what he or she has done. You can plead the blood over those people forgiving them and praying for mercy on them. Truly they require mercy because if they have sinned against you, God will judge them.

Mark 2: 2 They gathered in such large numbers that there was no room left, not even outside the door, and he preached the word to them. 3 Some men came, bringing to him a paralyzed man, carried by four of them. 4 Since they could not get him to Jesus because of the crowd, they made an opening in the roof above Jesus by digging through it and then lowered the mat the man was lying on. 5 When Jesus saw their faith, he said to the paralyzed man, "Son, your sins are forgiven."

This scripture talks about Jesus and that there were so many people gathered. There was no room for any more people. I have been to meetings like this my own self where there are thousands of people gathered to worship, praise and hear the Word of God. The largest meeting, I believe, I have been in is about 20, 000 people in a service. I know there are more. There are places in Africa they gather a million people or more; they use technology to broadcast and to project to all those people. Get yourself into some of those healing meetings or in with a people who believe the Word of God completely.

Examine your heart

Pray seeking God examining your own heart for any sin or offense within you. As the scripture teaches us to examine our hearts before communion so should we do regularly not just at communion. I would encourage you to examine your heart and take communion together as you seek divine healing. Make it a daily part of your life – communion with God. Offer yourself completely spirit, soul and body. Literally ask the Holy Spirit to bring it to you any sin or offense within you. Should something come to you, pray for forgiveness and ask God to cleanse you. Thank Jesus for forgiving you and for cleansing you. You only need pray once for forgiveness if you have truly repented.

1 Corinthians 11: 27 Therefore whoever eats this bread and drinks this cup of the Lord unworthily will be guilty of the body and blood of the Lord. 28 Let a man examine himself, and so eat of the bread and drink of the cup. 29 For he who eats and drinks unworthily, eats and drinks damnation to himself, not discerning the Lord's body. 30 For this reason many are weak and unhealthy among you, and many die. 31 If we would judge ourselves, we would not be judged. 32 But when we are judged, we are disciplined by the Lord, so that we would not be condemned with the world.

As Jesus gave Himself for your salvation, healing and deliverance, give your whole self to God. Hold nothing from Him. Surrender all yourself to God. Consecrating yourself in this way makes it possible for the Holy Spirit to fill you completely.

1 Thessalonians 5: 23 May the very God of peace sanctify you completely. And I pray to God that your whole spirit, soul, and body be preserved blameless unto the coming of our Lord Jesus Christ.

Literally offer your body as a vessel that God can use. God gave you the body to use on earth; thank Him and offer your body to God wholly. Give yourself to God and God will fill you with his presence. You may be healed instantly at that moment if you have never done what I am recommending you do.

Romans 12: 1 I urge you therefore, brothers, by the mercies of God, that you present your bodies as a living sacrifice, holy, and acceptable to God, which is your reasonable service of worship

Forgive

If God should bring to your spirit any offense or unforgiveness, you must forgive the person or people, no matter what they have done to you. As long as you have unforgiveness in your heart towards a person or people, there is like a stone in your heart, a hard spot that stops God's love from flowing through you the way a physical stone would stop your physical heart from functioning properly. We are commanded to forgive. We do not forgive because it wasn't anything much or because we were wrong etc. I mean even if you know without a doubt, injustice was done to you, you must forgive. Literally pray " In the name of Jesus Christ I forgive …name the person or people." Do it whether or not you feel like it. Do it because God commands us to do it. Do it by faith in Jesus blood. Hold no bitterness or resentment against anyone. Literally release it by faith in the blood of Jesus Christ. God is just and righteous.

If someone has abused you in some way, God will fight for you. You don't harbor any negative feelings towards the people. Please know it doesn't mean you should stay in an abusive situation of any kind. If you know an injustice was done to you, stay away from those people, but let God handle the situation. If we do not forgive, we will not be forgiven. I require forgiveness every day of my life. I know I need my Saviour Jesus. It's only by His blood I am holy.

Matthew 6: 14 For if you forgive men for their sins, your heavenly Father will also forgive you. 15 But if you do not forgive men for their sins, neither will your Father forgive your sins.

An Example of Unforgiveness

Peter though he was being generous with his offer of forgiving someone who offended him, but Jesus makes it clear, Peter is nowhere near what God expects of us. Jesus always forgives, so must we. In the example of the parable, a man begs for forgiveness and gets it. Promptly right afterwards he does not forgive someone who owes him money and throws him into debtors prison even though the man begs for mercy.

Matthew 18: 21 Then Peter came to Him and said, "Lord, how often shall I forgive my brother who sins against me? Up to seven times?"

22 Jesus said to him, "I do not say to you up to seven times, but up to seventy times seven.

23 "Therefore the kingdom of heaven is like a certain king who wanted to settle accounts with his servants. 24 When he began to settle the accounts, one was brought to him who owed him ten thousand talents.[b] 25 But since he was not able to pay, his master ordered that he be sold with his wife, their children, and all that he had, and payment to be made.

26 "So the servant fell on his knees, pleading with him, saying, 'Master, have patience with me, and I will pay you everything.' 27 Then the master of that servant was moved with compassion, released him, and forgave him the debt.

28 "But that same servant went out and found one of his fellow servants who owed him a hundred denarii.[c] He laid hands on him and took him by the throat, saying, 'Pay me what you owe.'

29 "So his fellow servant fell down at his feet and entreated him, saying, 'Have patience with me, and I will pay you everything.'

This is the spot in the parable where the person received forgiveness himself but became hard and did not forgive someone who owed him.

Matthew 18: 30 "But he would not and went and threw him in prison until he should pay the debt. 31 So when his fellow servants saw what took place, they were very sorry and went and told their master all that had taken place.

The original person the man owed money to hears of his wicked unforgiveness against someone who owed him much less. He revokes his forgiveness of the debt and places him in debtor's prison. In debtor's prison, people must come and pay to redeem you or you can never leave the prison. Often they work slave type hard physical labour. If no redeemer comes to pay your debt, you will never get out. Please know, Jesus Christ is our redeemer who paid the price for all sins. You receive his forgiveness freely, so must you forgive others. Let God take the care of it. Pray " I give you the care of the situation, you deal with the person" I have prayed that type of prayer, releasing unforgiveness and asking God to deal with the person, when it was someone I couldn't simply avoid. God knows how to deal with people who fight against his people.

Matthew 18: 32 "Then his master, after he had summoned him, said to him, 'O you wicked servant! I forgave you all that debt because you pleaded with me. 33 Should you not also have had compassion on your fellow servant, even as I had pity on you?' 34 His master was angry and delivered him to the jailers until he should pay all his debt.

35 "So also My heavenly Father will do to each of you, if from your heart you do not forgive your brother for his trespasses."

Mark 11: 22 Jesus answered them, "Have faith in God. 23 For truly I say to you, whoever says to this mountain, 'Be removed and be thrown into the sea,' and does not doubt in his heart, but believes that what he says will come to pass, he will have whatever he says. 24 Therefore I say to you, whatever things you ask when you pray, believe that you will receive them, and you will have them. 25 And when you stand praying, forgive if you have anything against anyone, so that your Father who is in heaven may also forgive you your sins. 26 But if you do not forgive, neither will your Father who is in heaven forgive your sins."

Claim the promise that God gave to Abraham over your own self. God will be your defense.

Genesis 12: 3 I will bless them who bless you
and curse him who curses you,[a]
and in you all families of the earth
will be blessed."

Even if you don't immediately "feel" like you have forgiven the person – thank God for cleansing you from unforgiveness. If it keeps bothering you, start praying over the person or people. You can find a scripture and pray it over him or her or them.

You can start praying a blessing over that person. That is pretty radical. Joyce Meyer prays for those who have said or done negative things to her, and sends them gifts. It is her way of keeping completely out of strife. She prays blessings over them The model she is following is Jesus Christ. Even from the horrible abuse he endured, although he did not sin, Jesus forgives in his dying moments.

Luke 23: 34 Jesus said, "Father, forgive them, for they know not what they do."

People of Like Precious Faith

There are some periods of your life, you might need to change your associations. It may only be temporary. It may be permanent. If in your spirit you know the person or people, are not believing or in any way helping you as you are believing for a miracle or healing, cut those people out of your life. I know it sounds serious because it is serious. IT could be a matter of your life or death. If someone is not helping you in your faith, keep them out of your life. The scripture below speaks of those of precious faith. I like King James that uses people of like precious faith – meaning you believe the same.

2 Peter 1: To those who have received a faith as precious as ours through the righteousness of our God and Savior Jesus Christ

If you cannot be in agreement with something as important as your health, you should not see those people. Keep them out of your life. Please know it may mean you will be alone more. When Jesus raised the dead, he cleared everyone out of the girl's room except her parents. On other occasions, when Jesus did a miracle, he only took Peter, James and John. He excluded the other disciples. Faith is essential in healings or miracles. You cannot have someone in disagreement or doubt who will not agree with you.

2 Corinthians 6: 14 Do not be unequally yoked together with unbelievers. For what fellowship has righteousness with unrighteousness? What communion has light with darkness? 15 What agreement has Christ with Belial? Or what part has he who believes with an unbeliever? 16 What agreement has the temple of God with idols? For you are the temple of the living God. As God has said:

"I will live in them
and walk in them.
I will be their God,
and they shall be My people."[b]
keep out unbelievers
keep out any hinderance to faith
only associate with those who encourage your faith

Words and Speech

I have briefly discussed the importance of confessions or what you say about yourself. It includes confessing God's Word over the physical situation. For instance, God's word states "by His stripes I am healed" Isaiah 53: 5. Do not agree with what is contrary to the word. The symptoms in your body may be manifesting, but you must agree with God's Word. I have been in prayer for people in life or death situations. The doctor's reports were bleak giving only a minimal chance of living. I could see these words pierce through my friends soul like a spear or an arrow. I knew I had to pray for her that God would encourage her with His Word. I would pray for words of wisdom and words of knowledge and discerning of spirits. I would pray long.

The Holy Spirit had me on a prayer assignment that lasted 2 years praying for a person to live rather than die. I knew it was not God's will for him to die. I would pray in the spirit; I would pray scriptures. I cut out of my life unnecessary entertainment and activities and focused on a miracle. It was my own free will choice to pray for my pastor's life. There were a small group of us who gathered for 2 years. More people would come and go; other people came occasionally etc. I knew it was God's prayer assignment for me. I did not want anything of unbelief in my life during that period.

My mouth began to come into agreement with God's Word concerning healing. If someone said anything negative, I would always bring a scripture that showed Jesus the healer. The people I associated with, the small group of believers all had the same heart about the matter. We were in complete agreement. There was unity in faith for complete and total healing of my pastor. It was not brief. We gathered in prayer every evening for 2 years. The 2nd year, he came home confounding the doctors' reports not only able to preach and teach but to jog and do sports activities.

If you need a healing or a miracle, you've got to align your words with what God says. Pray it. Say it. Believe it. Encourage yourself with it. Keep praising God for it. As long as necessary – it may be short or it may be long. The alternative may be death. I would rather believe all the way until I see the person healed.

I am not telling you not to get the best physicians and surgeons possible. God can use them. It is possible that they may not be Christians, and will not be sensitive as they give the information to the patient's loved ones.

My authority is higher than any authority on earth or in eternity. I directly go to God who created all things and who is the healer.

Words carriers of death or life – align with God's word

Spirit soul and body – command soul and body

If it is you who requires the healing, you may need your spirit to command your body to come into alignment. Listen to strong faith teaching and preaching to build your faith. Keep your heart believing. Get the best teaching and preaching possible and fill your life with it to keep your spirit strong.

Proverbs 23: 7 for as he thinks in his heart,
so is he.

Proverbs 4: 23 Keep your heart with all diligence,
for out of it are the issues of life.

Proverbs
18: 21 Death and life are in the power of the tongue,
and those who love it will eat its fruit.

Psalm 141: 3 Set a guard, O Lord, over my mouth;
keep watch over the door of my lips.

Psalm 19: 14 Let the words of my mouth and the meditation of my heart
be acceptable in Your sight,
O Lord, my strength and my Redeemer.

Christian Media – During that period while I was praying for my pastor's life, I mostly watched Christian media. I was discerning. I watched only things that encouraged my faith. I do believe God sharpened my discerning of spirits during that period because I would immediately know that something was worldly or unbelief and turn it off.

I got myself into alignment with the Healing Evangelists of the 20th century and read most of the books by John G. Lake, Maria Woodworth Etter, Aimee Semple McPherson and Smith Wigglesworth. Kenneth Hagin and Kenneth Copeland ministries were a refreshing to my spirit like cold water. I started giving to their ministries because they were imparting so much into my spirit. I didn't even know that it was scriptural to do it, I only knew I wanted to support them so that others could hear the good news about Jesus healing people. They encouraged my faith and strengthened me. Align yourselves with those who preach and believe in Divine healing.

Personal Relationship

It is necessary that you also keep your personal relationship with God. That must be your first priority. Pray, praise, worship. Read the Bible for your own spiritual growth. You must do it first. Next, pray for the healing or the miracle. Especially if it is a matter of life or death, give yourself to it as you would a job.

Give yourself wholly to it until there is healing manifested in the physical body. There have been many occasions I have seen or heard of doctors perplexed on how the disease was healed or why the person lived. Usually, they don't know what to say. A friend I prayed for on a different occasion had TB. It never completely goes away. It would have stopped her from being with the public. She was a minster of the gospel preaching to hundreds and hundreds of people; sometimes thousands. I gathered with friends who believed like I did that it was God's will to heal the minister completely. We met every day and prayed. We became very close during that period of our lives even though we had known each other many years. The connectedness in spirit was strong. That minister was completely healed. The hospital did not give her that report. The best they did is report that she certainly had TB on such and such a date and afterwards she had no sign of TB.

Use the healing testimony so that others might have faith. Share it with the people. As you do it gives God glory.

6 BELIEVE

Chapter 6 Do and keep doing until you receive your healing or miracle

Keep yourself right with God. Keep your relationship with God your priority. Be dressed spiritually in the armour of God. Spiritually you must keep built up and strong. By praying the armour of God over yourself each day, you pray strength over each part of your body. You are strengthening your spirit against any attack of the enemy. Victory in any area of life is possible for Christians who live in the spirit and use spiritual weapons. Our strength is not in any one other than The LORD Jesus Christ. It is through the strength of Christ that we can overcome. Literally praying the armour of God over yourself is as though you are putting on strength and protection.

Ephesians 6: 10 Finally, my brothers, be strong in the Lord and in the
power of His might. 11 Put on the whole armor of God that you may be
able to stand against the schemes of the devil. 12 For our fight is not
against flesh and blood, but against principalities, against powers, against
the rulers of the darkness of this world, and against spiritual forces of evil in
the heavenly places. 13 Therefore, take up the whole armor of God that you
may be able to resist in the evil day, and having done all, to stand. 14 Stand
therefore, having your waist girded with truth, having put on the breastplate
of righteousness, 15 having your feet fitted with the readiness of the gospel
of peace, 16 and above all, taking the shield of faith, with which you will be
able to extinguish all the fiery arrows of the evil one. 17 Take the helmet of
salvation and the sword of the Spirit, which is the word of God.

The helmet of salvation is the blood of Jesus applied to your life. It keeps you. Keep the word of God in your heart. The breastplate of righteousness covers your heart and internal organs. Keep yourself covered by the righteousness of Jesus Christ. The girdle of truth is like a belt of truth that covers you and protects your vulnerable areas. The shoes of peace mean you are walking in love and sharing the good news of salvation through Jesus Christ with others. I encourage you to believe you are truly placing these pieces of armour on your body as a protection of your spirit, soul and body. It is spiritual armour.

Rebuke the devil

Pray over yourself. " I bind you NAME THE DISEASE. You can have no place in me. I am washed in the blood of Jesus and Jesus died for my healing. I release angels to bring it to come to pass." If you are unsure about doing this part, get a mature minister of the gospel to pray it over you. It stops the attack on your body in the spirit realm and release God's angels to protect you.

Atmosphere for healing

There are different dimensions in the Spirit for healing. For instance, if you have been in a Benny Hinn healing Crusade, you will know there is going to be praise and worship and the most heaven like singing and worshipping of thousands of people. All of those people praising God together ignite the atmosphere for faith. Some people are healed as they are worshipping God. Some are healed during the preaching of the word. Others receive healing as people are giving their testimonies of healing.

There are other healing Evangelists with a different type of atmosphere. For instance, Rodney Howard Brown will have laughter and a spirit of joy so strong that people are released from sickness by the joy and laughter occurring. Gloria Copeland's healing school includes teaching and preaching on Jesus the healer and a quickening of faith to be strong to believe and receive healing. There are other passionate Evangelists who preach strong faith messages that cause there to be explosions of glory as they shout and praise Jesus for healing.

Healing can come in any of these ways and others. Healing may occur as you are quietly praying alone. It may occur as someone prays over you. It may occur in any place. The Evangelist Smith Wigglesworth would sometimes touch someone in faith on the street or in a bus or street car and impart healing. What I am saying is don't limit God. Don't place restrictions on how your healing will come. Pray and do all you can to strengthen your spirit first. Do what is necessary to keep yourself physically strong. Let the Holy Spirit lead you to the right place and the right people. "literally pray " Holy Spirit, lead me through this situation." And expect God to do it.

In your home, play praise and worship music and listen to uplifting faith preaching and teaching. Choose an area where you can pray and praise God where you will be free to praise, worship and read and confess scripture.

If your own Church does not move in the gifts of healing regularly, you must supplement your life with Christian Media and minsters who preach faith. What that means is those ministers are going to preach to you what God can do. They are going to quotes scriptures about believing God for healing and miracles. They are going to encourage you with positive messages.

If you know of a healing Evangelist or ministry in your town or nearby, go expecting God to meet you. Should you get the chance to get in a healing crusade, go and expect from God. Often being the presence of God with thousands of people all believing for healing and miracles ignites faith in those who come and helps to build their faith.

Write or type a list of healing scriptures and read them, pray them and confess them daily. Get scriptures on faith that will encourage your faith. Read those scriptures aloud. Pray them over yourself and believe them for your life.

Pray regularly with a spouse or family member or friend in agreement for you to receive your healing.

Pray over your own self stirring up gift of faith and gifts of healings and working of miracles.

Literally pray " I stir the gift of faith for healings and the working of miracles." Pray in tongues. Pray in English. When you pray in tongues, the Holy Spirit is praying for you exactly what is required. If you see a healing or miracle, rejoice with those who have received it. Realize that if God did it for them, he can do it for you also. Keep encouraging yourself with positive self-talk such as " God, you did it for them, I know your word is life. Thank you for my healing. Thank you for my miracle."

Sow to the spirit

Pray for others who need healing. Pray for others that need a miracle. As you sow spiritually into others, God will bless you for it. You may be sowing seeds of faith that will be quickened in you for your own healing. On more than one occasion, God has used me to encourage someone with positive words that later I realized were also words for myself. God can use you to speak blessings over others and also over yourself as you give to others.

Tithe

If you are not tithing, start. Give 1/10 of your income to your church or to the place that is your spiritual storehouse. It is God's commandment to give to the place that feeds you spiritually. God promises us that He will rebuke the devourer (the devil) and pour out a blessing so large, we don't even know how to receive it because it is so large.

Malachi 3: 10 Bring all the tithes into the storehouse, that there may be food in My house, and test Me now in this, says the Lord of Hosts, if I will not open for you the windows of heaven and pour out for you a blessing, that there will not be room enough to receive it. 11 I will rebuke the devourer for your sakes, so that it will not destroy the fruit of your ground, and the vines in your field will not fail to bear fruit, says the Lord of Hosts. 12 Then all the nations will call you blessed, for you will be a delightful land, says the Lord of Hosts.

Give above the Tithe

Sow financially into ministries that preach and teach healing and miracles and faith in God's Word as the final authority. As you do it, you are releasing your faith for those words to be imparted into your heart and life. Should you already be a partner with some of those ministries, pray for them; pray for the other partners; claim the blessings those ministries pray over their partners.

Thanksgiving and praise for God's Word – maintain it keep scripture in your eyes ears mouth.

Joshua 1: 7 Be strong and very courageous, in order to act carefully in accordance with all the law that My servant Moses commanded you. Do not turn aside from it to the right or the left, so that you may succeed wherever you go. 8 This Book of the Law must not depart from your mouth. Meditate on it day and night so that you may act carefully according to all that is written in it. For then you will make your way successful, and you will be wise. 9 Have not I commanded you? Be strong and courageous. Do not be afraid or dismayed, for the Lord your God is with you wherever you go."

Get as much Scripture as you can into yourself. I don't just mean any scripture. Faith building messages is what you require. Get them and play them over and over until the word is engrafted to your very soul (James 1: 21).

Healing scriptures CDS or DVDS

Either buy CD's or DVD's with healing scriptures on them or make your own. Read the scriptures into an audio recorder and play them over and over for yourself as you are doing ordinary things such as dishes or cleaning.

Positive - visualization of God's healing grace flowing through you.

See yourself whole and healed. Put some picture that cause you to believe for healing in a place you will see it. Put some item in a place where you can see it so it will be a reminder to you that God will provide. I'm not talking about anything that is weird. I am talking about giving yourself a focus to encourage your faith. It should be something that indicates God's healing strength towards you. I've known of people who place photos or pictures or clothing etc. that reminds them that God will heal them and that they will give God all the glory for doing it.

I myself like to put up scriptures in places I will see them every day such as in my car on the visor, or on the bathroom mirror. It is a place you will be reminded of God's mercy towards you.

Keep affirming your confession

Speak your confessing by praising God He is answering your prayers. Thank God for them.

1 Timothy 6: 12 Fight the good fight of faith. Lay hold on eternal life, to which you are called and have professed a good profession before many witnesses.

Keep thanking God

Make it a point to notice small things that bring you joy as well as other things that God has given you or done for you. Keep thanking God for all things you have received from Him. It releases joy in your spirit.

Psalm 77: 11 I will remember the works of the Lord;
surely I will remember Your wonders of old.
12 I will meditate also on all Your work

and ponder on Your mighty deeds.

Keep sowing and sowing and sowing to the spirit in these ways

In the region I live in, there are some crops you sow and keep sowing throughout the summer because they grow quickly such as carrots or lettuce. Keep sowing in faith believing for a harvest of healing in your life.

Ecclesiastes 11: 6 In the morning sow your seed,
and in the evening do not let your hand rest;
because you do not know which activity will find success,
this way or that way,
or if the both will be good.

Use your testimony to encourage others in their faith. Announce it at church. Write letters to ministries who prayed for you. Write a blog post. Post it to social media. Make a Utube video. If you do not know how to do these things, do everything that you can do to give God glory for your healing. Thank Him yes. Thank Him publicly. Thank Him so that He is glorified.

Conclusion

My book is a scriptural study of Divine Healing through God's mercy towards us. There are blessings to believers promised throughout the scriptures that include health and healing, long life, prosperity and protection. It is my prayer that you will have scriptural understanding of how it is God's will to heal you. It is God's will to prosper and protect you. Please be encouraged. Read, pray and confess the scriptures over yourself. Get into the company of believers who have faith for healing and miracles.

Hebrews 11: 6 And without faith it is impossible to please God, for he who comes to God must believe that He exists and that He is a rewarder of those who diligently seek Him.

PRAYERS

The following prayers are samples of prayers you could pray for important reasons. You could pray the same meaning in your own words. The prayers are meant as examples only.

PRAYER FOR SALVATION

Thank you- Jesus that you died for me on the cross. Thank you that you rose from the dead and ascended into heaven. Thank you that you are coming back again. I thank you Jesus for forgiving my sins. Thank you for your blood that cleanses me from all sin and unrighteousness. Thank you that your blood makes me holy. Thank you for saving me. Fill me with the Holy Spirit to overflowing. I pray for the baptism of the Holy Spirit. Lead me to other people who love you and serve you and that can help me know more about you. Give me the discerning of spirits strong. I thank you and praise you. With my mouth, I confess Jesus Christ is my LORD. Amen.

PRAYER FOR BAPTISM OF THE HOLY SPIRIT

Thank you- Jesus that you promised to send the gift of the Holy Spirit to us. Thank you that this promise is to all believers. I am a believer. I want all of you that you will give me. I want to know you God. Baptize me in the Holy Spirit with the evidence of speaking in other tongues. I believe you want to fill me to overflowing with your Spirit so that I might be an effective witness for Christ on the earth. Thank you for saving me. Thank you for your Holy presence. [begin praising God for what He has done for you – sing worship choruses and praise God in your natural language. Believe that He is present with you – start praising and worshipping Him. As phrases come to you in other tongues, say them – praise God with new tongues.] I praise you. I thank you. I receive the baptism of the Holy Spirit.

PRAYER FOR RELEASING ANGELS

God, I thank you that angels are ministering spirits sent as ministers to us. I pray over my prayer request NAME IT HERE. God I pray release angels to perform it. I thank you for releasing the answer to me. I praise you for it. Amen.

PRAYER FOR RESISTING EVIL

I am the redeemed of the LORD. Jesus Christ has saved me. I am a new creation in Christ Jesus. Jesus blood covers me. I live in the spirit. The Holy Spirit of God fills my spirit. O Holy Spirit quicken me; give me wisdom. Pray [expecting God will give you discerning of spirits so you will have the right words to speak.]

In the name of Jesus Christ, I bind you. I rebuke you evil spirit. In the name of Jesus, I command you to go out. You have no place in my life. I cast you out. You have no place with me. I am covered by the blood of Jesus and His righteousness is my righteousness. Go out evil spirit in the name of Jesus Christ!
Thank you, Holy spirit for your holy presence. Release angels to drive out the enemy. Thank you. Amen.

PRAYER FOR PROTECTION

Holy Spirit release angels to protect me. I plead the blood of Jesus over me. I pray the protection you promise to your people. Cover me Jesus. Holy Spirit give me wisdom, discernment and understanding. Thank you for angels that guard over me. Thank you for your blood that protects me and a hedge of protection around me. I praise you O God. [praise God with some worship choruses and expect God's holy presence to be manifest in you]. Thank you. O God for protection.

PRAYER FOR HEALING

Lord Jesus, Thank you that you gave your life for me so that I can be saved, healed and delivered. I thank your for the scripture that by your stripes I am healed. I thank you for my healing.

NAME THE DISEASE I bind you in the name of Jesus. I cast you out. I pray over myself that I would be whole spirit, soul and body.

Thank you God for your healing manifestation in my life. I give you all the glory. Amen.

SCRIPTURES ON HEALING

This is not a complete list. I encourage you to search the scriptures yourself to find scriptures on healing. There are excellent books and CDS you can purchase that have many healing scriptures on them. I have only included this to be a resource. If possible, read the scriptures into an audio recorder so you can play them to yourself; hearing God's word will release faith.

I have often taken each scripture one by one and personalized for example

" Thank you that I abide in the secret place of the most high"(Psalm 91)... You could do that with each one of the scriptures, as a guide to help you pray healing for yourself.

Exodus 15: 26 He said, "If you diligently listen to the voice of the Lord your God, and do what is right in His sight, and give ear to His commandments, and keep all His statutes, I will not afflict you with any of the diseases with which I have afflicted the Egyptians. For I am the Lord who heals you."

Isaiah 53: 4 Surely he has borne our grief
 and carried our sorrows;
Yet we esteemed him stricken,
 smitten of God, and afflicted.
5 But he was wounded for our transgressions,
 he was bruised for our iniquities;
the chastisement of our peace was upon him,
 and by his stripes we are healed.

Isaiah 61: 61 The Spirit of the Lord God is upon me
 because the Lord has anointed me
 to preach good news to the poor;
He has sent me to heal the broken-hearted,
 to proclaim liberty to the captives,
 and the opening of the prison to those who are bound;
2 to proclaim the acceptable year of the Lord
 and the day of vengeance of our God;

to comfort all who mourn,
3 to preserve those who mourn in Zion,
to give to them beauty
for ashes,
the oil of joy
for mourning,
the garment of praise
for the spirit of heaviness,
that they might be called trees of righteousness,
the planting of the Lord,
that He might be glorified.

Psalm 30: 2 O Lord my God, I cried to You,
and You healed me.

Psalm 103: 1 Bless the Lord, O my soul,
and all that is within me, bless His holy name.
2 Bless the Lord, O my soul,
and forget not all His benefits,
3 who forgives all your iniquities,
who heals all your diseases,
4 who redeems your life from the pit,
who crowns you with lovingkindness and tender mercies,
5 who satisfies your mouth with good things,
so that your youth is renewed like the eagle's.

Psalm 107: 20 He sent His word and healed them
and delivered them from their destruction.

Psalm 118: 17 I shall not die, but I shall live
and declare the works of the Lord.

Psalm 147: 3 He heals the broken in heart,
and binds up their wounds.

Proverbs 3: 3 My son, do not forget my teaching,
but let your heart keep my commandments;
2 for length of days and long life
and peace will they add to you.

Proverbs 3: 16 Length of days is in her right hand,
and in her left hand riches and honor.

17 Her ways are ways of pleasantness,

Proverbs 4: 20 My son, attend to my words;
incline your ear to my sayings.
21 Do not let them depart from your eyes;
keep them in the midst of your heart;
22 for they are life to those who find them,
and health to all their body.
23 Keep your heart with all diligence,
for out of it are the issues of life.

James 5: 13 Is anyone among you suffering? Let him pray. Is anyone merry?
Let him sing psalms. 14 Is anyone sick among you? Let him call for the
elders of the church, and let them pray over him, anointing him with oil in
the name of the Lord. 15 And the prayer of faith will save the sick, and the
Lord will raise him up. And if he has committed any sins, he will be
forgiven. 16 Confess your faults to one another and pray for one another,
that you may be healed. The effective, fervent prayer of a righteous man
accomplishes much.

1 Peter 2: 24 He Himself bore our sins in His own body on the tree, that
we, being dead to sins, should live unto righteousness. "By His wounds you
were healed."[

3 John 2 Beloved, I pray that all may go well with you and that you may be
in good health, even as your soul is well.

Romans 10: [d] This is the word of faith that we preach: 9 that if you
confess with your mouth Jesus is Lord, and believe in your heart that God
has raised Him from the dead, you will be saved, 10 for with the heart one
believes unto righteousness, and with the mouth confession is made unto
salvation.

Acts 2: 38 Peter said to them, "Repent and be baptized, every one of you, in
the name of Jesus Christ for the forgiveness of sins, and you shall receive
the gift of the Holy Spirit. 39 For the promise is to you, and to your
children, and to all who are far away, as many as the Lord our God will
call."

Acts 3: 16 And His name, by faith in His name, has made this man strong,
whom you see and know. And faith which comes through Him has given
him perfect health in your presence.

Acts 4: 8 Then Peter, filled with the Holy Spirit, said to them, "Rulers of the people and elders of Israel: 9 If we today are being examined concerning a good deed done to a crippled man, how this man has been healed, 10 be it known to you all, and to all the people of Israel, that by the name of Jesus Christ of Nazareth, whom you crucified, whom God raised from the dead, by Him this man stands before you whole.

Exodus 20: 12 Honor your father and your mother, that your days may be long in the land which the Lord your God is giving you.

Deuteronomy 11: 8 Therefore you must keep all the commandments which I am commanding you today, so that you may be strong and go in and possess the land which you are going to possess; 9 and that you may prolong your days in the land which the Lord swore to your fathers to give to them and to their descendants, a land flowing with milk and honey.

1 John 1: 9 If we confess our sins, He is faithful and just to forgive us our sins and cleanse us from all unrighteousness.

1 John 2: 2 My little children, I am writing these things to you, so that you do not sin. But if anyone does sin, we have an Advocate with the Father, Jesus Christ the Righteous One. 2 He is the atoning sacrifice for our sins, and not for ours only, but also for the sins of the whole world.

Deuteronomy 30: 9 The Lord your God will make you prosper in every work of your hand, in the offspring of your body, and in the offspring of your livestock, and in the produce of your land, for good. For the Lord will once again rejoice over you for good, just as He rejoiced over your fathers, 10 if you obey the voice of the Lord your God, by keeping His commandments and His statutes which are written in this Book of the Law, and if you return to the Lord your God with all your heart and with all your soul.

Acts 10: 38 how God anointed Jesus of Nazareth with the Holy Spirit and with power, who went about doing good and healing all who were oppressed by the devil, for God was with Him.

Naaman the Leper

2 Kings 5: 14 So he went down and dipped himself in the Jordan seven times, according to the word of the man of God, and his flesh returned like the flesh of a little boy, and he was clean.

King Hezekiah

2 Kings 20: 4 Now before Isaiah had come out of the middle courtyard, the word of the Lord came to him, saying, 5 "Turn back and say to Hezekiah the leader of My people: Thus says the Lord, the God of David your father: I have heard your prayer; I have seen your tears. I will heal you. On the third day, you shall go up to the house of the Lord. 6 I will add to your days fifteen years, and I will deliver you and this city from the hand of the king of Assyria. I will defend this city for My own sake and for the sake of David My servant."

Healing of the Shunamite woman's child

2 Kings 4: 32 When Elisha came into the house, he saw that the boy was dead, lying on his bed. 33 So he went in, and shut the door on the two of them, and prayed to the Lord. 34 He went up and lay on the child, put his face on his face, and his eyes on his eyes, and his hands on his hands. Then he bent over the child, and the child's flesh warmed. 35 Then he got down, walked once back and forth in the house, and went up, and bent over him; the boy sneezed seven times, and the boy opened his eyes.

Acts 19: 11 God worked powerful miracles by the hands of Paul. 12 So handkerchiefs or aprons he had touched were brought to the sick, and the diseases left them, and the evil spirits went out of them.

Matthew 28: 18 Then Jesus came and spoke to them, saying, "All authority has been given to Me in heaven and on earth. 19 Go therefore and make disciples of all nations, baptizing them in the name of the Father and of the Son and of the Holy Spirit, 20 teaching them to observe all things I have commanded you. And remember, I am with you always, even to the end of the age." Amen.

John 4: 43 After the two days He departed from there and went to Galilee. 44 For Jesus Himself testified that a prophet has no honor in his own country. 45 Then, when He came to Galilee, the Galileans welcomed Him, having seen all the things He did at Jerusalem at the feast. For they had also gone to the feast

46 So Jesus came again to Cana of Galilee where He had made the water wine. And there was a certain nobleman whose son was sick in Capernaum. 47 When he heard that Jesus had come out of Judea into Galilee, he went to Him, pleading that He would come down and heal his son, for he was at

the point of death.

48 Then Jesus said to him, "Unless you see signs and wonders, you will not believe."

49 The nobleman said to Him, "Sir, come down before my child dies."

50 Jesus said to him, "Go your way. Your son lives."

John 5: 5 After this there was a feast of the Jews, and Jesus went up to Jerusalem. 2 Now in Jerusalem by the Sheep Gate there is a pool, which in Hebrew is called Bethesda, having five porches. 3 In these lay a great crowd of invalids, blind, lame, and paralyzed, waiting for the moving of the water. 4 For an angel went down at a certain time into the pool and stirred up the water. After the stirring of the water, whoever stepped in first was healed of whatever disease he had. 5 A certain man was there who had an illness for thirty-eight years. 6 When Jesus saw him lying there, and knew that he had been in that condition now a long time, He said to him, "Do you want to be healed?"

7 The sick man answered Him, "Sir, I have no one to put me into the pool when the water is stirred. But while I am coming, another steps down before me."

8 Jesus said to him, "Rise, take up your bed and walk." 9 Immediately the man was healed, took up his bed, and walked.

John 9: 9 As Jesus passed by, He saw a man blind from birth. 2 His disciples asked Him, "Rabbi, who sinned, this man or his parents, that he was born blind?"

3 Jesus answered, "Neither this man nor his parents sinned. But it happened so that the works of God might be displayed in him. 4 I must do the works of Him who sent Me while it is day. Night is coming when no one can work. 5 While I am in the world, I am the light of the world."

6 When He had said this, He spat on the ground and made clay with the saliva. He anointed the eyes of the blind man with the clay, 7 and said to him, "Go, wash in the pool of Siloam" (which means "Sent"). So he went away and washed, and returned seeing.

John 11: 43 When He had said this, He cried out with a loud voice, "Lazarus, come out!" 44 He who was dead came out, his hands and feet wrapped with grave clothes, and his face wrapped with a cloth.

Jesus said to them, "Unbind him, and let him go."

Matthew 18: 19 "Again I say to you, that if two of you agree on earth about anything they ask, it will be done for them by My Father who is in heaven. 20 For where two or three are assembled in My name, there I am in their midst."

Mark 2: 8 Immediately, when Jesus perceived in His spirit that they so reasoned within themselves, He said to them, "Why do you contemplate these things in your hearts? 9 Which is easier to say to the paralytic: 'Your sins are forgiven you,' or to say, 'Rise, take up your bed and walk'? 10 But that you may know that the Son of Man has authority on earth to forgive sins," He said to the paralytic, 11 "I say to you, rise, and take up your bed, and go your way to your house." 12 Immediately he rose, picked up the bed, and went out in front of them all, so that they were all amazed and glorified God, saying, "We never saw anything like this!"

Luke 8: As He went, the people crowded Him. 43 And a woman having a hemorrhage for twelve years, who had spent all her living on physicians, but could not be healed by anyone, 44 came behind Him, and touched the fringe of His garment. And immediately her hemorrhage dried up.

45 Jesus said, "Who touched Me?"

When everyone denied it, Peter and those who were with Him said, "Master, the crowds are pressing against You, and You say, 'Who touched Me?' "

46 But Jesus said, "Someone touched Me, for I perceive that power has gone out from Me."

47 When the woman saw that she was not hidden, she came trembling. And falling down before Him, she declared to Him before all the people why she had touched Him and how she was healed immediately. 48 Then He said to her, "Daughter, be of good cheer. Your faith has made you well. Go in peace."

Luke 8: 50 But when Jesus heard it, He answered him, "Do not fear. Only believe, and she will be made well."

51 When He came into the house, He permitted no one to go in except Peter, John and James, and the father and mother of the girl. 52 All wept and mourned for her. But He said, "Do not weep. She is not dead but sleeping."

53 They laughed at Him, knowing that she was dead. 54 But He put them all outside and took her by the hand and called, saying, "Little girl, arise." 55 Her spirit returned, and she arose immediately. And He told them to give her food. 56 Her parents were astonished, but He commanded them to tell no one what had happened

Mark 16: 15 He said to them, "Go into all the world, and preach the gospel to every creature. 16 He who believes and is baptized will be saved. But he who does not believe will be condemned. 17 These signs will accompany those who believe: In My name they will cast out demons; they will speak with new tongues; 18 they will take up serpents; if they drink any deadly thing, it will not hurt them; they will lay hands on the sick, and they will recover."

Matthew 17: 14 When they came to the crowd, a man came to Him and knelt before Him, saying, 15 "Lord, have mercy on my son, for he is an epileptic and suffers terribly. He often falls into the fire and often into the water. 16 I brought him to Your disciples, but they could not heal him."

17 Then Jesus answered, "O faithless and perverse generation, how long shall I be with you? How long shall I bear with you? Bring him here to Me." 18 Jesus rebuked the demon, and he came out of him. And the child was healed instantly.

Luke 5: 12 When He was in a certain city, a man full of leprosy, upon seeing Jesus, fell on his face and begged Him, "Lord, if You will, You can make me clean."

13 He reached out His hand and touched him, saying, "I will. Be clean." And immediately the leprosy left him.

14 Then He commanded him to tell no one, "But go and show yourself to the priest and make an offering for your cleansing, as Moses commanded, as a testimony to them."

15 Yet even more so His fame went everywhere. And great crowds came together to hear and to be healed by Him of their infirmities. 16 But He withdrew to the wilderness and prayed.

Acts 3: 3 Now Peter and John went up together to the temple at the ninth hour, the hour of prayer. 2 A man lame from birth was being carried, whom people placed daily at the gate of the temple called Beautiful to ask alms from those who entered the temple. 3 Seeing Peter and John about to go into the temple, he asked for alms. 4 Peter, gazing at him with John, said, "Look at us." 5 So he paid attention to them, expecting to receive something from them.

6 Then Peter said, "I have no silver and gold, but I give you what I have. In the name of Jesus Christ of Nazareth, rise up and walk." 7 He took him by the right hand and raised him up. Immediately his feet and ankles were strengthened. 8 Jumping up, he stood and walked and entered the temple with them, walking and jumping and praising God. 9 All the people saw him walking and praising God. 10 They knew that it was he who sat for alms at the Beautiful Gate of the temple. And they were filled with wonder and amazement at what happened to him.

Hebrews 11: 6 And without faith it is impossible to please God, for he who comes to God must believe that He exists and that He is a rewarder of those who diligently seek Him.

Romans 10: 17 So then faith comes by hearing, and hearing by the word of God.

Deuteronomy 11: 18 Therefore you must fix these words of mine in your heart and in your soul, and bind them as a sign on your hand, so that they may be as frontlets between your eyes. 19 You shall teach them to your children, speaking of them when you sit in your house and when you walk by the way, when you lie down, and when you rise up. 20 You shall write them on the doorposts of your house and on your gates, 21 so that your days and the days of your children may be multiplied in the land which the Lord swore to your fathers to give them, as long as the days of heaven on the earth.

Luke 17: 11 As Jesus went to Jerusalem, He passed between Samaria and Galilee. 12 As He entered a village, there met Him ten men who were lepers, who stood at a distance. 13 They lifted up their voices, saying, "Jesus, Master, have pity on us!"

14 When He saw them, He said to them, "Go, show yourselves to the priests." And as they went, they were cleansed.

Mark 8: 22 He came to Bethsaida. And they brought a blind man to Him and entreated Him to touch him. 23 He took the blind man by the hand and led him out of the town. When He had spit on his eyes and put His hands on him, He asked him, "Do you see anything?"

24 He looked up and said, "I see men as trees, walking."

25 Then again He put His hands on his eyes and made him look up. And he was restored and saw everyone clearly. 26 He sent him home away to his house, saying, "Neither go into the town, nor tell it to anyone in the town."

Luke 4: 40 Now when the sun was setting, all those who had anyone sick with various diseases brought them to Him. And He laid His hands on every one of them and healed them. 41 And demons came out of many, crying out, "You are the Christ, the Son of God!" But He rebuked them and did not permit them to speak, because they knew that He was the Christ.

Matthew 10: 10 He called His twelve disciples to Him and gave them authority over unclean spirits, to cast them out, and to heal all kinds of sickness and all kinds of disease.

Matthew 10: 2 Now the names of the twelve apostles are these: first, Simon, who is called Peter, and Andrew, his brother; James, the son of Zebedee, and John, his brother; 3 Philip and Bartholomew; Thomas, and Matthew, the tax collector; James, the son of Alphaeus; and Lebbaeus, whose surname was Thaddaeus; 4 Simon the Zealot; and Judas Iscariot, who also betrayed Him.

Matthew 10: 5 These twelve Jesus sent out, and commanded them, saying, "Do not go into the way of the Gentiles, and do not enter any city of the Samaritans. 6 But go rather to the lost sheep of the house of Israel. 7 As you go, preach, saying, 'The kingdom of heaven is at hand.' 8 Heal the sick, cleanse the lepers, raise the dead, and cast out demons. Freely you have received, freely give.

Matthew 28: 18 Then Jesus came and spoke to them, saying, "All authority has been given to Me in heaven and on earth. 19 Go therefore and make disciples of all nations, baptizing them in the name of the Father and of the Son and of the Holy Spirit, 20 teaching them to observe all things I have commanded you. And remember, I am with you always, even to the end of the age." Amen.

Acts 5: 12 Many signs and wonders were performed among the people by the hands of the apostles. And they were all together in Solomon's Porch. 13 No one else dared join them, but the people respected them. 14 Believers were increasingly added to the Lord, crowds of both men and women, 15 so that they even brought the sick out into the streets and placed them on beds and mats, that at least the shadow of Peter passing by might touch some of them. 16 Crowds also came out of the cities surrounding Jerusalem, bringing the sick and those who were afflicted by evil spirits, and they were all healed

Acts 20: 10 Paul went down and leaned over him, and embracing him said, "Do not be troubled, for he is alive." 11 When he had gone up and had broken bread and eaten, he conversed for a long while until dawn and departed. 12 They took the lad in alive and were greatly comforted.

Acts 9: 32 The Healing of Aeneas

32 As Peter passed through every region, he came down also to the saints who lived in Lydda. 33 There he found a man named Aeneas, who had been bedridden for eight years and was paralyzed. 34 Peter said to him, "Aeneas, Jesus the Christ heals you. Rise up and make your bed." And immediately he rose up. 35 All those who lived in Lydda and Sharon saw him and turned to the Lord.

Acts 9: 6 In Joppa there was a disciple named Tabitha, which is translated Dorcas. This woman was full of good works and almsgiving. 37 In those days she became ill and died. And when they had washed her, they placed her in an upper room. 38 Since Lydda was near Joppa, the disciples, hearing that Peter was there, sent two men to him, pleading, "Do not delay to come to us."

39 Peter rose up and went with them. When he arrived, they led him into the upper room. All the widows stood by him weeping, and showing the tunics and garments which Dorcas had made while she was with them.

40 Peter put them all outside and knelt down and prayed. And turning to the body he said, "Tabitha, arise." She opened her eyes, and when she saw Peter she sat up. 41 He gave her his hand and lifted her up. And when he had called the saints and widows, he presented her alive. 42 It became known throughout all Joppa, and many believed in the Lord. 43 He remained in Joppa for many days with Simon, a tanner.

Acts 28: 7 In that area was an estate of the chief man of the island, named Publius, who had welcomed us and courteously housed us for three days. 8 It happened that the father of Publius lay sick with a fever and dysentery. Paul visited him and, placing his hands on him, prayed and healed him. 9 When this happened, the rest on the island who had diseases also came and were healed. 10 They honored us in many ways. And when we sailed, they provided us with necessary supplies.

Leviticus 22: 17 The Lord spoke to Moses, saying: 18 Speak to Aaron, and to his sons, and to all the children of Israel, and say to them: Whoever from the house of Israel or from the foreigners in Israel who offers his burnt offering for any vows or freewill offerings that he offers to the Lord, 19 then if it is to be accepted for you, the offering shall be a male without blemish, a bull, sheep, or goat.

Thanksgiving offering

Leviticus 22: 29 When you offer a sacrifice of thanksgiving to the Lord, offer it so that it may be accepted. 30 On the same day it shall be eaten. You shall leave none of it until the next day: I am the Lord.

Romans 10: 17 Consequently, faith comes from hearing the message, and the message is heard through the word about Christ.

Deuteronomy 28: 2 All these blessings will come on you and accompany you if you obey the LORD your God: 3 You will be blessed in the city and blessed in the country.
4 The fruit of your womb will be blessed, and the crops of your land and the young of your livestock—the calves of your herds and the lambs of your flocks.
5 Your basket and your kneading trough will be blessed.
6 You will be blessed when you come in and blessed when you go out.
7 The LORD will grant that the enemies who rise up against you will be defeated before you. They will come at you from one direction but flee from you in seven.

1 Thessalonians 5: 23 May the very God of peace sanctify you completely. And I pray to God that your whole spirit, soul, and body be preserved blameless unto the coming of our Lord Jesus Christ.

Romans 12: 1 I urge you therefore, brothers, by the mercies of God, that you present your bodies as a living sacrifice, holy, and acceptable to God, which is your reasonable service of worship

Matthew 6: 14 For if you forgive men for their sins, your heavenly Father will also forgive you. 15 But if you do not forgive men for their sins, neither will your Father forgive your sins.

Genesis 12: 3 I will bless them who bless you
and curse him who curses you,[a]
and in you all families of the earth
will be blessed."

Proverbs 23: 7 for as he thinks in his heart,
so is he.

Proverbs 4: 23 Keep your heart with all diligence,
for out of it are the issues of life.

Proverbs
18: 21 Death and life are in the power of the tongue,
and those who love it will eat its fruit.

Psalm 141: 3 Set a guard, O Lord, over my mouth;
keep watch over the door of my lips.

Psalm 19: 14 Let the words of my mouth and the meditation of my heart
be acceptable in Your sight,
O Lord, my strength and my Redeemer.

Ephesians 6: 10 Finally, my brothers, be strong in the Lord and in the power of His might. 11 Put on the whole armor of God that you may be able to stand against the schemes of the devil. 12 For our fight is not against flesh and blood, but against principalities, against powers, against the rulers of the darkness of this world, and against spiritual forces of evil in the heavenly places. 13 Therefore, take up the whole armor of God that you may be able to resist in the evil day, and having done all, to stand. 14 Stand therefore, having your waist girded with truth, having put on the breastplate of righteousness, 15 having your feet fitted with the readiness of the gospel of peace, 16 and above all, taking the shield of faith, with which you will be able to extinguish all the fiery arrows of the evil one. 17 Take the helmet of salvation and the sword of the Spirit, which is the word of God.

Joshua 1: 7 Be strong and very courageous, in order to act carefully in accordance with all the law that My servant Moses commanded you. Do not turn aside from it to the right or the left, so that you may succeed wherever you go. 8 This Book of the Law must not depart from your mouth. Meditate on it day and night so that you may act carefully according to all that is written in it. For then you will make your way successful, and you will be wise. 9 Have not I commanded you? Be strong and courageous. Do not be afraid or dismayed, for the Lord your God is with you wherever you go."

1 Timothy 6: 12 Fight the good fight of faith. Lay hold on eternal life, to which you are called and have professed a good profession before many witnesses.

OTHER BOOKS BY CHRIS LEGEBOW

Available on Amazon.ca Amazon.com or Amazon.ca or Kindle
Or the Create Space webstore.

Living Word Publishers

Angels: Ministering Spirits

An Excellent Spirit: Living Life Wholly Unto God

Covenant With God: God's Relationship With Man

Discovering and Using your Spiritual Gifts

Divine Healing in the Scriptures: God's Mercy Towards Man

The Doctrine of Christ: Essential Truths of Scripture

The Five-Fold Ministry: Gifts to the Church

Kinds of Prayer. Knowing Them and Using Them Effectively

Living Life Fully: Knowing your Purpose

The Anointing: the Glory of God

The High Calling: Life Worth Living

The Sacraments: A Charismatic Guide

ABOUT THE AUTHOR

Chris Legebow is a Christian Professor of English and Communications. She has taught at the elementary, high school and College and University levels. She has ministered in her local churches in intercessory prayer, teaching Sunday school and other Christian Doctrine classes to children and youths. She has preached to congregations and given her testimony. Although she was not raised in a Christian home, she came to know Jesus Christ as her Saviour and LORD while she was studying in University. This radically transformed her life in terms of priorities and commitment. She has a strong passion for the great commission – that Jesus Christ would be preached throughout all the earth believing that it a major sign of the LORD's return. She has been a part of several different types of full gospel charismatic churches but has also gained much of her insight and enlightenment from Christian Media and broadcasting. She hopes to continue ministering, serving, interceding and giving and teaching until the LORD returns.

www.ingramcontent.com/pod-product-compliance
Lightning Source LLC
Chambersburg PA
CBHW021205020426
42331CB00003B/209

* 9 7 8 1 9 8 8 9 1 4 0 2 2 *